WILDFIRE

A Memoir

Karrah Youngblood

KARRAH
YOUNGBLOOD
publishing

Published by Karrah Youngblood.

Use of the F word: 58 times.

Apologies to my aunts: once—right here.

Contents

For my mother—

who gave me her strength, even after she was gone.

For my offspring—

the reason I kept going.

For Amie—

who gave me my thick skin the way only a big sister can.

For Christen, Marci, & Heather—

the best friends I never asked for.

For the SLS & #23—

for being my rock through this writing process.

For the survivors of Jason Lewis—

this one was always for you.

For the family, friends, co-workers, and random strangers who supported me along the way—

I'm forever humbled and grateful.

For RJ's daughter—

and for everyone else's daughter. And for their daughters too.

May you grow up in a world that believes you.

"...silence like a cancer grows."

—Paul Simon

Foreword

Cross-examining the man who beat and raped me wasn't something I ever imagined would show up on my life's Bingo card. After all, I'm not even an attorney. But there I was, standing in an old courthouse in Pawnee County, Oklahoma, face to face with a monster. A man who left a trail of battered wives and girlfriends in his wake, thriving on the destruction of innocent women.

This is a classic David vs. Goliath scenario.

How did it come to this? Me, a single mom, standing in court without a lawyer, staring down a man who thought he could beat me, rape me, and silence me. He glared at me with those cold, black eyes so often seen in psychopaths, but I didn't flinch. I glared right back.

It was the first and only time I ever had the chance to ask my abuser everything I wanted the world to know about him. Every cruel act he had ever committed against a woman weighed on me, but instead of crushing me, it fueled me. He wanted to jump the bench and choke me. He couldn't, though—he was in front of a judge this time.

It all started with a flyer. An 8.5" x 11" piece of paper I created to warn others about the serial abuser lurking in their neighborhood. A desperate act of survival. A warning. A rebellion. And that flyer ignited something far bigger than I ever could have imagined—something still unfolding in real time.

Yet here I was, silenced by the system, but still speaking. Silenced by my abuser and by the systemic failures that protected him at every turn, as well as my own failures. Fighting back against a man who wasn't just *my* monster, but a monster to so many others. A man who tried to crush me—and almost succeeded.

I wasn't here to lose.

The truth is protected by the First Amendment of the United States, and I am in the business of telling it.

I hope my story inspires you to share my truth, your truth, and all truth—like wildfire.

Disclaimer: *Some names and identifying details have been changed to protect the innocent—and to protect me from further legal abuse at the hands of a serial predator. The events in this book are true. And while some names are altered, let's be honest: it's not exactly a hard Google if you're trying to connect the dots.*

Trigger Warning: *This memoir includes depictions of abuse, domestic violence, sexual assault, and other forms of trauma that may be distressing to some readers. Please proceed with care.*

Quick Note for the "What About Men?" Crowd: *Yes, men can be victims too. Abuse doesn't care about gender. But let's talk numbers: 1 in 4 women will experience severe physical violence from a partner. 1 in 3 women will face some form of intimate partner violence. And when a woman is murdered? There's a good chance it was by someone who "loved" her. This book isn't about denying male pain. It's about focusing on the fire that's burning hottest. And right now, that's women being failed—loudly, publicly, and repeatedly—by the system meant to protect them.*

If that makes you uncomfortable, good. Lean in.

Our first date was to be at Silver Dollar City, an 1800s themed amusement park in Branson, Missouri, where we would also stay the weekend, maybe see a show, eat good food, the fun cheesy date stuff. I was so excited. I hadn't been on a date in years, and here I was being absolutely spoiled. We talked all the way there. It's a little over 200 mile drive, and we took our time, stopping at Truck Stops just to shop through their goofy gift racks. As pathetic as it sounds, I remember being excited he put gas in my car. It had been a decade since someone paid for my gasoline, so I remember feeling taken care of immediately. *It's the little things, right?*

We bought trucker hats, cheap sunglasses, "anything I wanted" so of course I cashed that promise in for some beef jerky. We talked all the way there about anything and everything. He told me all about his sister that committed suicide, and how he helps raise his nieces and goodness I felt sorry for him. He was really going through an ugly custody battle and his ex wife was just an awful woman. Having so many women after his money, he could genuinely see that I had good intentions, and that it was his personality that was attractive to me.

Not only did he have one ex-wife (Maggie) giving him custody battle fits, and threatening to move out of state with his beloved daughters, his *other* ex-wife was the one he REALLY had to worry about. Sharon Lewis was obsessed with her ex-husband, and did not take the divorce well. She stalked him at all hours of the night.

his law degree that he didn't even use, and was a savvy powerful businessman that could often be overheard closing massive deals. After Googling him immediately, I discovered that he owned a light up t-shirt company that had a contract with the Dallas Mavericks and Houston Rockets. Jason Lewis was unlike any man I had ever met. He was tall, strong, decisive, adventurous, and he truly swept me off my feet that late September of 2014.

He found me on Facebook. His son was in the same high school class as my niece, and we had been texting and FaceTiming regularly for a week, so he seemed trustworthy enough to agree to a whirlwind first date out-of-state. My kiddo was at her grandparents' for the weekend, and life is short, right? I had a little orange Chevy Sonic that got good gas mileage, so I insisted we drive it. I picked him up and met him for the first time in his driveway in his pseudo upscale neighborhood.

Jason Lewis was above six foot, stocky, and carried himself with such a badass disposition, it was hard not to be taken aback. There was a cocky aire about him that rocked my good judgment to its core. I was buying what he was selling. I was smelling what he was stepping in. I think it is safe to say that, despite my playing hard to get, he really had an instantaneous hold over me. I could definitely see how he fathered a baby with Country Music singer Sara Evans. This man was so cool.

Chapter One

The Love Bomber

"Nothin' lasts forever, and we both know hearts can change." — Guns N' Roses, "November Rain"

He wasn't even that good looking, but he was sharp—and I liked sharp. At the time, I was in the thick of it: somewhere in my mid-thirties, raising my seven-year-old daughter, Rayne, caring full-time for my handicapped dad, and juggling two demanding roles at a family-owned music company in Tulsa. I was their in-house graphic designer and a fully booked piano teacher, teaching dozens of students every week. Every hour of my day was spoken for—and then some. If a man was going to keep up with my life, he had to be extraordinary.

Jason Lewis seemed exactly that.

He and his daughters lived in a gorgeous two-story house a few miles away, he owned a plane and had his pilot's license, he had

I was not a jealous person, so I had no reason to be threatened by any of these ladies. I just legitimately felt sorry for him because he was truly a victim of bad luck with women. I guess I didn't realize how hormonal and possessive women could be until I met Jason and heard his horror stories. *Why on earth would they both behave so childishly? Why don't they just let him move on and enjoy his life with his daughters that he just loves with all of his bones? Why couldn't they have just been cool and easy to get along with like me?*

You see, within hours of meeting him, I was already ready to prove myself as the Unicorn. The cool chick that loves hard, laughs loud, has a smart mouth but is kind and colorful. "Are you my Unicorn?" he asked before we ever got to the hotel. God for some bizarre reason, I wanted to be. Without even realizing it, I was already in a competition with his crazy ex wife. "She won't be a problem," he promised.

Because I was insisting on not being a slut and sticking to my five date rule, he was a gentleman and got us a hotel room with two beds. I didn't want to get separate rooms, because I wanted to get to know him, but I did not want to share a bed that first night, even if he was Prince Charming. I may cuss like a shitfaced sailor, but I do pride myself in being a "good girl."

After we made it to our our hotel room that he secured with his mother's debit card (the first real red flag I noticed), I needed to pee, which meant walking past him to go to the bathroom. That's when

I felt his hand hit my ass harder than my Mom or Dad ever thought about. Tears welled up in my eyes immediately. It surprised me more than anything. Scared me a little. I'd never been hit that hard in my life—and now I was 200 miles from home with a man who thought that was perfectly fine.

I tried to hide my tears and composed myself behind the closed door of the bathroom. After I flushed the toilet, and re-entered the room, he noticed my mascara had been running and asked me in a condescending voice, something like "You aren't crying are you? I barely touched you. I did not hurt you, don't be a crazy bitch please."

I didn't want to be a crazy bitch.

It didn't really hurt that bad.

I was behaving like a baby.

Why am I being so emotional?

Was my blood sugar low?

I'm tough. I'm a unicorn.

I went to my car, smoked a joint to clear my head, and that's when he came to my car and begged me to come back inside so we could go to dinner. So I did.

As he changed in front of me out of his roadtrip clothes and into something to wear to the restaurant, I noticed a large tattoo between his shoulder blades—two thick black Roman columns: "II." "That's for Jason Lewis the Second," he said. "My son has a matching one—his says 'III.' We got them in Rome when he was in High School. Matching father-son tattoos."

I actually thought that was endearing. Sweet, even. And the idea of him someday taking me to Rome? That was already painting little daydreams across my pea-brain canvas.

Jason was pouty at dinner and I was on eggshells, so I decided to get shitfaced. That bothered Jason too.

After a very contentious dinner, Jason performed a complete 180° and was so wonderful for the rest of upright parts of the night. I even agreed to sleep in the same bed and cuddle. But not long after I fell asleep with a smile on my face, I was woken up with his hand in my pajama bottoms. I told him "no" but he continued. I was so sleepy and drunk, I didn't want to deal with the fallout of saying "no" so I had sex with him. I broke my own rule. I honestly don't remember it. I do remember his unusually small dick, and wondering how that poor man functioned with such a small organ. *(Remember, the truth is protected by the First Amendment.)*

The next morning, we got up early and headed to Silver Dollar City. I hadn't been there since I was a kid, and gosh I felt like one that morning. In retrospect, it's fitting we were headed to ride roller coasters, seeing how my whole trip had felt like one so far. It was truly one of my favorite places to visit as a child with my cousins, so I was more than ready to ride some water rides. We had a wonderful day. He was a little handsy, but it wasn't the worst. We rode rides until I was sick, and had a fun day eating kettle corn and watching glassblowers. One thing he said that stood out to me was "See how they are looking at us? They already think we are married." He was really making sure I knew how comfortable he was with me, and I was simply having too much fun to see that this man was already slowly chipping away at my dignity.

For example, he was taking a picture of me with my phone, but wouldn't give it back unless I milked a fake cow. I love it when people tease me, I take it as a sign of affection, and I was honestly laughing in hysterics at myself milking the black and white wooden adorable bovine with rubber nipples. That laid-back fun-filled fall day was the first time he even joked about taking my phone away from me, but it certainly wasn't the last. *More on that in a minute.*

That evening back at the hotel wasn't so great. He was waving around the largest red flag I had ever seen, and there I was in the Ozark Mountains of Missouri ignoring it like it was potato salad. I hate potato salad. After falsely accusing me of being engaged to my gay male co-worker, he walked in the bathroom as I was drying my hair and decided to hit my ass again, only this time with his belt. I had never been hit with a belt in my life, and I was truly in shock. In tears, I packed my things, walked downstairs to my car and started it.

I wish like hell I could yell to the girl I was then and say "leave his ass there, Karrah!" I sat there in my running car crying and confused.

If I left I would have ruined our weekend. *It was salvageable right?* If I had driven away that night, I wouldn't have eventually become a resident expert on domestic violence.

He talked me into staying there another night and was full of deep tear jerking apologies. We slept in separate beds, and after he accused me of being the worst snorer he's ever heard, we got up super early and headed home. This trip was over. This relationship was over before it started.

Why do I still want to be his Unicorn though? The further we got away from our hotel, the nicer he got. He started to play music, we were singing, laughing, and I was really starting to enjoy myself again. *There is just something extra about this man that I love being around.*

We made it back to Oklahoma, and I was still having a grand ole time, despite the multiple bright red flags he was throwing my way. Flags such as "I have retroactive jealousy" and "I get kinda grumpy when I'm drinking" and "I'm a stalking victim." Looking back, I was just excited to be away for the weekend. I was so stoked to just have a break from being a mom and a caregiver, that his red flags were being ignored left and right.

Jason had several places he really wanted to show me, and my daughter was excited to spend another night at her grandparents' so we extended our whirlwind first date another night. He wanted to take me to the town where he grew up and give me the full tour of the land he was about to purchase. After filling an ice chest full of his favorite Clamato beers, the tour began. Our stops included Frog Rock (a big rock that looks like a frog) where he insisted on taking a picture of me. Next we ended up on a little beach called "Sandy Point", a place he used to love to go party with his friends. As we made our footprints in the ugly decorated-with-trash Keystone Lake sand, he rambled to me about all of the different projects he has in the works. He told me all about his personal assistant Vicki Brochan and how she would be great for helping me market my designs. I immediately connected with the beautiful young girl on Facebook. Jason was already helping me try to make money for myself. He was trying to empower me. It was fascinating how intelligent he was. He was one of a kind—*lucky me*. Even though he had a thick Oklahoma accent, he seemed so foreign. Like I said, this man was sharp, and to me, sharp was hot.

We next visited his mother's house in his hometown of Cleveland, Oklahoma. Cleveland was a little run down town just thirty miles west of Tulsa. His mother was not at home, so I was relieved to not have to meet her on our first date. His mother's place was nothing like the house Jason owned in the neighboring town. It seemed like such a success story to see how far he had come. He spoke of wanting his mother to move to a nicer home, but she loves it there and refuses to leave. The house was honestly just plain and small, and it gave me the creeps. The little 800 square ft house was located in the middle of the small town, just by the high school and a stone's throw from

Billy Vessels Park. It had a short gravel driveway, was unimpressive, and was filled with the weirdest shit you've ever seen. From the dozens of Jesus dolls on the shelves to a massive wall-sized portrait of 16-year-old mullet-clad Jason above the bed in his old bedroom, everything felt like it was staring at me. His mattress was pushed against the wall, which had a window unit air conditioner in it. The ceiling made noises because there had to be rats and squirrels living somewhere between the roof and the half wall that separated his mother's room.

Burning red flag on that one, Youngblood.

The house was decorated with Jason's awards for Outstanding Salesmanship, and one titling him "Best Christian Character Award" from a Christian School he attended as a child. I do remember thinking that was rather adorable and it gave me reassurance that he couldn't have been a bad guy. By then, I found out he was a Deacon at the church down the street. We weren't at his mother's odd little house for long, thank goodness.

Our next stop really tugged me in the feels. We were within a mile from the cemetery where his sister was buried. "Would you mind if we stopped for a quick visit?" he asked. Of course I didn't mind going by and seeing his sister's grave. This poor man was still grieving his only sibling, of course we could go fluff the flowers on her headstone while we were in the neighborhood.

After we parked in the grass of the Cleveland Cemetery, we got out of my car and walked through a sea of headstones directly to a modest plot in the northern section of the burial ground. Never once did it occur to me that I was standing in the middle of a graveyard with one of the most vicious men to ever walk among us. I was just sorry for his loss.

It was complicated because toward the end of her life, according to Jason, his sister Catey had lost her mind. I was actually surprised when he used the words, "crazy bitch" when he described her behavior in the days before her death. He had told me not to be a crazy bitch in the hotel room. *He must really like using that term.* Jason's sister tragically ended her life by hanging herself with a rope tied in two precise knots to cut off her airways. It surprised me when he told me that he had once co-owned a funeral home business with his late sister, which meant he was also the one who embalmed her, arranged her funeral, and picked out her headstone. I felt so sorry for him to have to go through all of this, and I was impressed he had a Master's Degree that he failed to mention. *Red flags all around, Karrah Jo. He embalmed his fucking sister.*

After a short visit with the dead, he insisted on me meeting his nieces. "They would simply adore you because you'll remind them of their mother." That one hit me right in the heart. I felt so sorry for those girls I had never even met, having had to bury their mother too soon. He drove me to their house, where they lived with their father, a successful Chiropractor. Nobody was home, but Jason had full run of the place, so he took me on a tour of this massive house out in the middle of nowhere that once belonged to his big sister. I could see that his whole family clearly had money, not that I was after that. I just could tell I was dealing with a family that had a lot of drive for success.

Drive is hot.

As we toured the estate, I pretended to be impressed. I may have grown up humbly on a farm in Oklahoma, but I had a few rich family members, including my dad's brother who lived across the street from John Elway, during the time he was Quarterback for the Denver Broncos. I didn't want to hurt Jason's feelings by mentioning the fact that my mom's house was much larger than this one and her sister's house probably doubled it, so I just pretended to care about the square footage.

Why is he so braggy? How cute he's trying to impress me. Does he not realize I'm an art nerd and I could care less about money and things?

Next, he guided me into a room with a grand piano. The piano's lid was closed and covered in dust so it clearly hadn't been played in a while. "That was my sister's piano. Sit down and play it." I felt weird sitting down on the bench, but it was a piano, and I loved playing the piano, so I agreed. I poured all nine minutes of "November Rain" into that off-key piano, his eyes fixed on me like I was something he couldn't quite figure out. Then we left.

It was late afternoon as we were leaving the big empty house, we were only a few miles from my parents' new farm house that had plenty of room upstairs. By then, part of me just wanted to be around my Momma. My mother had been suffering from Early Onset Alzheimer's for years. My stepdad took care of her every day and made sure she was able to live out the rest of her life at home, only getting a caregiver break once a day from the hospice nurses he religiously made cookies for. By that stage of my mom's advanced illness, I was making a weekly visit to see my parents. Even though I was still technically on a first date, I think I deep down just wanted a safe place to sleep where I could control my situation. Jason agreed to go stay at my parents' for the night but first he wanted to take me to one more place. His favorite place.

Boston Pool Road.

Boston Pool Road is a gravel country road out in the middle of nowhere. It extends about 8 miles long, making a full circle loop around several thousand acres of Typical Oklahoma land, filled with deer stands and oil leases. You see, this was Jason's place of reflection. This is where he got away from the grind of being a successful businessman.

This is where he came to just drive.

Around an 8-mile circle.

Over and over and over again.

This wasn't a sober affair either. It turns out, Jason's favorite way of letting off steam was to have a few beers and circle Boston Pool Road until his head was clear, and then he would leave. He called it "Dirt Road Therapy" or "Booze Cruising" later on.

"Some men like to fish, I like to drive country roads," he said.

I could buy that, I was driving anyway, so I didn't care if he drank. There weren't exactly any police officers patrolling in the middle of the country, so I wasn't worried about the open containers. I was not drinking, so I at least knew I wouldn't get a DUI. I felt like such a rebel having open containers in my car. *Afterall, I am on a weekend getaway right? I'm also a goddamn unicorn.*

I remember wanting so badly to just hurry so we could go see my Mom before it was her bedtime, but deep down I was already afraid of making this man mad. *(I'm sorry, can you move that red flag? I can't see to drive.)* After our third trip around, he told me to pull over just a little up ahead because he wanted to show me one thing before we left to go to my parents' house. We climbed through a metal gate that was just a few feet off the road, and walked up a dirt tire trail through some weeds toward the edge of a cliff that overlooked a body of water below. He pointed across the reddish brown muddy surface of the Arkansas river, "Do you see that?"

Across the river was the back part of my parents' land. I couldn't see her house from the trees, but I could see a familiar landmark. This Boston Pool Road property he was wanting to purchase was a canoe ride from my ailing mother and her beautiful 80 acre horse farm. We were a heartbeat away from the bed that I carved my name in as a kid and my stepdad's margaritas.

How lovely would it be to live there?

It seemed like the perfect Unicorn field to me. While I was not having thoughts of moving in with him on our first date, he really threw me off by hinting about it. *This man likes me so much he's already talking about giving me land?* Sure, I don't like things, and I'm not after people's money. Land is a different story. Land was gold to me because they weren't making any more of it. Land by my dying mother was platinum. *Who was this man, and why can't I think straight?* No one has ever talked this much about a future with me since high school. I was starting to feel oddly special.

It was already getting dark when we left Boston Pool Road for the short jaunt to my parents' farm. As we drove up the long driveway, my mom's beautiful three-story recently built modern farmhouse came into view. This was not the house that I grew up in, but it felt like home since my Mom and Stepdad were there. They sold the 100 acre farm I grew up on and moved a few counties away to build my mother's dream home. I'm not sure why they built such a huge house, but it sure was beautiful. My mom started to get sick with Alzheimer's just after they purchased the land, but she was still very hands-on in building and decorating her home. Nestled all cutelike on top of a hill, from the upstairs window you could see for miles.

It had a wrap around porch for sunrise and coffee or to enjoy one of Robert's famous mason jar margaritas on the screen door Summer evenings. Salted rim and everything. Jason wasn't impressed with ANY of it.

Even though the size of my parents' house seemed to bother him, he was still on his best behavior. I'm not sure why it wasn't a big deal to introduce him to my Stepdad, but it just didn't occur to me it was still a first date. My mom was very advanced in her illness at the time, was on home hospice, and her hospital bed was in the middle of the living room. One of my biggest regrets to this day in all of this story was introducing Jason to my Mom. She was laying there, still beautiful but frail, and that look of recognition I could always see in her eyes didn't let me down. There she was, finally realizing her baby daughter was standing there beside her. She even said "Hi" to Jason.

I'm sorry mom.

I gave her a kiss and then she drifted off into her usual blank stare. These familiar vacant expressions had become longer and longer over the years, and I was tired, so I wanted to go upstairs and go to bed. As we got up, Jason Lewis leaned over and gently kissed my mom's forehead right there in front of God and everybody. *Fucking weird.* Even for me then it was weird, but I just chalked it up as him having a big heart. *Puke.*

I don't remember exactly how that long weekend of a first date ended, but I know this: it was the start of a ride I wasn't ready for.

Over the next three weeks, Jason would chip away at me piece by piece, until I barely recognized the girl he'd met. But at the time, I didn't see the crash coming—I was still caught up in the thrill of the ride.

The morning after we had got back from our blur of a first date, and I was back at the music school waiting for my first class to start, I got a Facebook message from a woman claiming to be Jason's girlfriend. Her name was Christen Norris. According to her, they were very much together. According to Jason, she was just some poor girl who couldn't take a hint. "She's obsessed with me," he said. "I've never let her out of the friend zone."

I wanted to believe him—so I did. Christen and I exchanged a few spicy messages on Messenger, nothing too wild, but just enough to get the blood pumping. She was pissed. I was smug. I didn't give it much thought beyond that, honestly. It didn't make me worried—it just fired up the competitor in me.

He's mine, you delusional twit. I'm the one he's with. I'm the unicorn. I fart rainbows and sparkle under pressure. I have absolutely no reason to question this man's intentions.

She blocked me after that exchange.

And me? I had some rainbow-colored crop dusting to do.

The second weekend I spent with Jason Lewis, he had managed to absolutely ruin the ever living shit out of my 36th birthday. After promising me a nice dinner and a night in, all started out as planned. He even got me a birthday cake with candles. Unfortunately Jason had a bad day preparing for his custody case, so he wanted to go drive around Boston Pool Road to "clear his head". At first I wasn't fine with that, but Jason threw a tantrum and threw a barstool through the glass door of his oven, barely missing me, and I quickly stopped whining. So that's what we did on my 36th trip around the sun, drove around in a circle. Over and over again. After we got back to his house and he passed out, I woke up in his daughter's bed with the excruciating pain of having his grossness shoved in my ass. I felt a tear immediately. *I'm actually not sure how, seeing he was so small.* Then when he couldn't stay hard, he started to use a glass beer bottle. It seems he doesn't just drink Clamatos since they only come in cans. This was a brown glass beer bottle. I don't remember what happened after that, I just remember feeling so much shame. *I guess I just rationalized that if I'm going to get the kind of man that takes care of me, I'm going to have to be a little tougher and crazier in the sack. I came to the conclusion that I probably did something to deserve this.* After he fell asleep, I gathered my things and drove the short drive to my house, where I cried in the shower until I ran out of hot water. Here I was in that typical movie scene after the girl gets raped, scrubbing off her body like she can never get his filth off. I was that girl. The happy, outgoing, bubbly Karrah was dead in just two short weeks.

So why did I date him for three weeks?

This is the age old question that I finally got answered: Why women go back to their abusers.

The answer is because they can apologize and bomb you with so much "love" you can't see straight nor remember the abuse from the night before, and Jason was a master at this craft. (*I can still barely remember that night.*) Jason was good. He was real good. He even promised me he would stop drinking through real tears. Women go back because they want to recapture that moment in the beginning when everything was wonderful. Part of me wanted to go back to when we laughed ourselves breathless riding water rides in the Ozark Mountains. Part of me wanted to go back to that moment when he pointed across the water to my mom's land, like we were building some kind of future together. But deep down, I already knew I wasn't going back for good. I knew that Jason Lewis and I didn't have a future at this point—but this man had hurt me, and I didn't want to be so devastatingly wrong about someone. I had already spoken so highly of him to some of my family. I didn't want to eat crow. I didn't want to admit that this man I had introduced to my child was abusive. After all, I had carved pumpkins with his daughters and my kid just adored them—and they adored her right back. During one of those nights, sometime between the second and third weekend, we had a weeknight Jack O'Lantern-carving date with our kids. I sat outside and scraped pumpkin guts with his girls and my daughter, while Jason sat inside, pouting about something. His youngest daughter even made me a necklace and told me sweetly, "I hope you marry my dad." And during that time, I met his mother, Pam. She was warm, friendly—almost convincing. She sold me the story that Sharon and Maggie, the two women Jason was fighting in court, were completely batshit crazy. They weren't wonderful and warm like me, according to Pam. Poor Jason, she said, was just a victim of these women's drama. And for a moment, I believed her, even though he had already physically harmed me. *I am still very ashamed of that fact.*

Somewhere in that blur—maybe a weeknight I've blocked out—we watched the movie *Divergent* in his bed.

Hang tight. We'll circle back to that in a minute.

The third and final weekend with Jason Lewis started on Boston Pool Road where he drank Banana Schnapps (his "Panty Remover Drink") and Clamato beers. About the second trip around this 8 mile shithole of a road, he finally shut the fuck up so I had some time to think. *What am I doing with this piece of shit man?* Then something just hit me. The tough country girl that I've always been had finally re-entered my body.

This date is over, I'm taking him home, and I'm done.

That mentality caused him to point his handgun at me and forced me to stop my car. I'm sure I was petrified out of my mind, but I remember rationalizing for the first of many times, "*this man can't kill me, everyone will know it was him.*" Deep down, I was not scared for my life, even though looking back, I most certainly should have been. We got in an altercation that ended with him trying to choke me with my seatbelt and slamming my head into my windshield, cracking the glass instantly.

I was still determined to get home.

I pulled off Boston Pool Road onto the pavement county road, and that's when his next fit began. He threw a raging childlike tantrum all the way to my home town of Sapulpa, around 45 miles worth. The whole time, as I was driving, I just let him rant, sometimes interjecting a smartass remark.

He can't hurt me, I'm driving the car he's riding in, right?

As we were getting closer to his house, I started to get more brave and a little more mouthy. I'm not sure what it was I said, but he immediately stuck his thumb in my mouth and pulled my cheek so hard it separated from my gums. I finally was able to keep my smart mouth shut for a minute after he finally stopped. That shit hurt.

Driving 55 miles per hour, exactly the speed limit so we didn't get pulled over and get caught with his open containers, we only had about three miles left until we got to his house when he made that familiar phone threat I had remembered from our first date. That's when he told me, "I am going to take your phone and put you in a field somewhere so nobody can find you all weekend." He knew my sister could track my location, and was making sure I knew she wouldn't be able to find me.

Jeez.

Instead of being scared like I should have been, I smarted off, "How are you going to kidnap me when I'm the one driving? Why don't you drink a little bit more?" That's when I found out I had underestimated the amount of absolute batshit crazy in this man. As I was behind the wheel of my car, driving in the dark on a four lane major highway, driving 55 miles an hour, it happened.

His fist hitting the side of my face felt like a hammer.

I remember the initial shock of the absolute insanity of Jason punching the person driving him down the road, and the utter horror that it was me. Still to this day, I'm not sure how I managed not to swerve, or even cross into the other lane, but that was the exact moment that I learned something huge about myself: *I have an undeniable ability to keep my cool.* I then threatened to call the police, and that's when he humbled me hard with his words. He glared at me with those black eyes he got when he turned into the monster, and said "I will kill your daughter if you tell the police. No questions asked, Cunt. If you tell the police, I will lose my kids, and it's an eye for an eye bitch." There it was. He was threatening to murder my only child, and I truly believed he was capable of doing so. My hands trembled on the wheel as I processed this information. Several scenarios ran through my head and they all ended with the horrible graphic vision of my daughter covered in blood. *What would I ever do without her? What kind of mother would I be if my bad taste in men ended my child's life?*

My overly creative brain was on overdrive. There was no way in absolute batshit hell I was going to tell a cop what he did to me. No fucking way, José. I was too scared to tell a single soul, much less a uniformed officer.

After dropping him off at his house just moments later, that was the last time I saw Jason Lewis outside of a courthouse.

Chapter Two

Fake Smile, Real Bruises

"I'm shutting down the negativity, I'll find the optimist in me." — Evie Irie, "The Optimist"

I was one of the lucky ones. I got out of my tumultuous relationship with Jason Lewis in just under 21 days, but I knew deep down I would never be the same. I was confused about what had just happened to me, and a million thoughts ran through my mind about what I did to deserve his abuse. I downplayed it all in my head: *Was it really that bad?*

It was like the atrocious things he did never fully registered in my hard head. It was as if I hadn't been walking around with a butthole that needed a doctor's attention, wearing maxi pads for weeks so I wouldn't bleed on my piano bench. All I could recall clearly was how kind and captivating he *could* be when he wasn't drinking. I didn't want this roller coaster of emotions to end up being all for nothing.

Even if I was intimidated into not telling the police that I'd been beaten and raped by my ex-boyfriend, I did, however, tell my sister and my boss the *partial* real reason we broke up. I had separate, uncomfortable conversations with both of them—crying through the safer details, leaving out the worst parts. I hadn't even said the worst of his acts out loud to *myself* yet. I felt too humiliated to admit them. Not only did I carry the shame of having been violated, but I also walked daily with the guilt that I had done nothing about it. I didn't stand up for myself. I was *so* ashamed to have put myself in that position.

The little girl me would be so disappointed in the big girl me.

Looking back, I can't believe I swallowed enough pride to tell my sister Amie and Kim, the Vice President of Saied Music Company, about those horrific three weeks with Jason. I'm a tough farm kid, known for my smart mouth and constant grin—*what the hell was I thinking? Why did I settle for that, even if it was only three weeks?*

Suddenly, I empathized with every girl in history who did not report her abuser. In that moment, I believed every victim in the world. I could relate to anyone wearing sunglasses over bruised eyes, making excuses for him in my head. I truly believed that Jason hurting me was my fault, something I'd done wrong. I was powerless. Hell, I even emailed him after he threatened my child's life. Thinking about that still makes me sick to my stomach. I will carry that shame to my deathbed, but the truth is, this man had me in a psychological chokehold. At the time, I still thought he was a business genius (more on that later) and wanted to somehow benefit from my horrible experience, so I asked him via email if he could help me get my Adult Beginner Piano Classes onto cruise ships. *(I still stand by my idea—Carnival, call me!)* I don't remember exactly what our emails said, but it was clear I was showing signs of Stockholm Syndrome for months after our abrupt split. That might sound over-the-top for a relationship shorter than a typical Christmas break, but it's true, and later a therapist confirmed it. Three weeks with Jason gave me full-on PTSD and Stockholm Syndrome. He was a master at getting inside people's heads.

Part of me wanted to *fix* him, to help him be the man I thought he could be if only he was loved by the *right* girl. I naively believed I was that girl. That was when I learned I have a ridiculous amount of empathy for others but needed to work on my own self-respect. Also, looking back, during that period of my life I didn't have the self confidence to be alone. I thought I needed someone to go through life with.

The email exchanges through late 2014 started out cordial—but they always went south faster than a porta-potty at a chili cook-off. At first, he played nice, tossing around polite sentences and thinly veiled condescension like he was still trying to maintain the upper hand.

But it never took long before he reverted to the same manipulative tone he always used: smug, slippery, and full of shit.

He had this knack for rewriting history in real time. I'd bring up the fact that he hurt me—physically, emotionally, psychologically—and he'd twist himself into an Olympic-level gaslighting pretzel to convince me it never happened. Or that I wanted it. Or that I was confused. Or dramatic. Or broken. You know, the usual grab bag of narcissistic rebuttals. The greatest hits.

"Oh, I touched you?" he once wrote, like it was some distant, abstract concept instead of the violent, soul-splitting reality it had been. Yeah. He touched me. That motherfucker touched me in ways no man ever should—ways I still feel in my bones, even now. And let me tell you, there's no typo big enough to undo that kind of imprint.

But even when it was just a reply on a screen—even when my hands shook after hitting send—it felt good to respond. To name it. To stand up to him, even in font size 11. It was like microdosing my own courage. A tiny act of defiance. A tiny flame licking back toward the hand that tried to snuff me out.

And every time I stood up for myself in those emails, it was like I was inching my voice out of the corner he'd shoved it into. Line by line, I was reclaiming power he thought he still had. He didn't.

Looking back, my job saved me. My piano students saved me. Teaching adult recreational beginner piano classes at Saied Music Company, even while sad, turned out to be one of the best medicines. Music made me happy; it makes everybody happy—that's a scientific fact. I remember walking into my office that Monday with a broken soul and makeup covering my bruised cheek and eye.

How am I supposed to be bubbly today?

Mondays were my full days: an adult beginner class at 10 a.m., a teen class at 4 p.m., another adult class at 6 p.m., plus private lessons scattered throughout the day. We had a Halloween showcase coming up, and I was also in charge of designing store graphics. I faked my smile as best I could.

I was semi-honest with my adult classes, telling them I'd broken up with my boyfriend and was having a rough day. Since it was the first time they'd seen me down, they showed so much concern that it made me feel loved. I needed that love. They tried everything to cheer me up; one student, Belle Adams, a 70 something grandmother, came back after her lesson with my favorite sugary Starbucks drink. Another, Rebecca Jones (a CPA in her 50s), gave me a hug only a mother can give you until I stopped crying. Larry Zimmer, a retired Oil and Gas Executive who took lessons along with his wife, baked me a strawberry rhubarb pie after class with a note that read something like, *"Sorry you're having a bad day. Chin up, kid. —Larry."*

They had no clue how much they were carrying me through the toughest time of my life.

At home, I slipped right back into my roles: caregiver, single mom, household ringmaster. There was no room for a breakdown, no time to curl up and unravel. Dinner still needed to be made, the dogs still needed to be fed, the bills still needed to be ignored until payday. Life didn't pause just because I'd been thrown off a cliff and landed in a heap of bruises and humiliation.

Thankfully, he hit me on a weekend. I know how twisted that sounds—"thankfully"—but it bought me a couple of days. My daughter was at her dad's, and I had a little window to ice my face, piece together a version of the story that didn't make me feel like human garbage, and figure out how to show up on Monday pretending everything was fine.

When Rayne walked in the door from her dad's that Sunday evening, I let her know Jason and I were done.

She shrugged and just said "okay."And honestly, she looked relieved.

She didn't need the details. Not then. She was too young to carry the weight of what that man did to me. I carried it instead. Quietly. Wrapped in layers of shame and barely-held-together pride.

Telling my dad? That was a whole other brand of dread. I'd bragged about Jason like I was bringing home a trophy—smart, charming, successful. A man, finally, who seemed to want me. I had sold him so hard that now the return policy felt humiliating. What was I supposed to say? *"Hey, remember that guy I practically issued a press release about? Yeah, turns out he's a monster. My bad."*

I just... didn't tell him. I let the silence speak for me. Let the subject quietly dissolve, like spoiled leftovers nobody wanted to mention.

Was that immature? Probably. But I was bruised, bone-deep, and shame is a hell of a silencer.

By day three back at work, my chin was up and staying there. At least on the outside. I made a choice to be happy every morning, literally saying "Thank" and "You" the second my feet hit the floor. I believe the Universe can do cool things when you exude gratitude, and cool things indeed started happening. I got asked to be on the *Tad and Lindsay Show*, a local morning radio program, giving pumpkin-carving tips to callers. (This would be an excellent time to inform the reader that I'm also a professional pumpkin carver. A legitimate one.) Then I was hired to carve pumpkins with the Tulsa Chamber of Commerce as a team-building exercise. Next, Cox Communications paid me to carve two Jack O'Lanterns for legendary college football coaches Barry Switzer and Pat Jones—and I got to watch a game with them. Anyone in Oklahoma knows what a big deal that is. Here I was, hanging out with one of Jason's heroes, storing Barry Switzer's phone number in my cell.

Hell yes, I was.

After that, I carved a *Charlotte's Web* pumpkin for my daughter's first-grade class and had a wonderful Halloween with my little vampire. Of course, I was still looking over my shoulder, knowing what he was capable of, but my "bounceback" was noticeable. That was one more thing I loved about myself, even if I still felt as ugly and fat as Jason told me I was. While my mental mindset was trying to find its way back to normal, physically, my body immediately began to pack on the pounds. I didn't even care or notice at the time. Survival mode doesn't exactly care about waistlines. My body just did what it needed to do to stay afloat while my brain tried to untangle the wreckage.

Thanksgiving at my parents' house was wonderful. I helped my stepdad cook, played several games of pool upstairs with Rayne, and found myself belly-laughing with my sister. It was safe to say my comeback was in full swing. By Christmas, I'd won tickets to see Justin Timberlake through a local radio contest. My student Belle had crocheted blankets for me and my child. And my boss, Kim, went on 6 In The Morning—a local morning show—where she promoted my adult beginner piano classes and introduced me to the entire Tulsa metro as "The Amazing Karrah Youngblood." It's hard to stay sad when your employer compares you to Spider-Man on the morning news. *Maybe it was a defense mechanism, getting so cocky after nearly being destroyed by a douchebag, but by early 2015, I was convinced Spider-Man didn't have shit on me.*

Even though I'd clawed my way back to something that resembled happiness, that gnawing need to make sense of it all never really left me. I still needed answers. I still needed justice. And let's be honest—I still needed to mentally shiv that son of a bitch for what he did.

Closure? Maybe. Revenge? Also yes.

By January of 2015, the rage had started to calcify into strategy. So I did what any woman with unresolved trauma and a black belt in sarcasm might do: I poked the fucking bear.

Now don't worry—I wasn't trying to see him, talk to him in person, or breathe his godawful Copenhagen breath. But I was ready to confront him through the safe, glowing screen of my iPhone. I wanted him to know he hadn't walked away clean. That he didn't get to clock women and ride off into the goddamn sunset like some misunderstood antihero with a dark past and a weak jawline.

It's honestly hilarious that I thought I could appeal to his conscience—like maybe, just maybe, there was a sliver of human decency buried under that meat suit and rotten tomato beer stink.

Nope.

He fired back instantly with a photo of his new girlfriend—an objectively stunning woman, poor thing—and a verbal punch to my girly parts, calling me a fat-ass and a waste of time.

I didn't flinch. I wrote back, "She's beautiful, Jason. I hope you don't beat her."

And that was the moment I realized: I wasn't under his spell anymore.

I didn't want him to think I was healing—I wanted him to worry. I wanted him to squirm at the thought of me not staying quiet. At the thought that one day, I might tell someone what he did.

And that maybe, just maybe, someone would believe me.

Then came that message—pure venom, chilled and gift-wrapped in misogyny. The kind you save for a rainy day... or a District Judge.

"You will know her soon through Rayne, and she's not a cunt like you, so no beatings required."

He claimed she worked at my daughter's elementary school.

The impact of him admitting—however twisted—that he'd hurt me was huge. It was the closest thing to proof I'd gotten. A breadcrumb. A loaded sentence I could hand over to someone in power if I ever grew the cojones to step forward.

So I did what survivors do when the system doesn't: I filed that shit away.

I screenshotted the email, opened my laptop, and created a folder titled "Monster."

Karma loves receipts.

Chapter Three

CHRISTEN

"But to tip the score, it sometimes takes just one." — Regina Spektor, "One Little Soldier"

Spring 2015. Six months out of Jason's orbit and I was still walking around like I'd just survived a car crash no one saw happen. Sure, I was finding glimpses of happiness on occasion, but I couldn't quite get back to the girl I was before I met Jason. I had made my way out of that bizarre fever dream he called a relationship, and donned a grin most days, but I was still very raw deep down. Not just emotionally—I'm talking scorched-earth, twitchy-at-loud-noises raw. I was disoriented some days, humiliated, and still trying to decode the wreckage he left behind. Physical and emotional abuse turns everything sideways until you can't tell what's real anymore. Trauma doesn't exactly hand you a user manual.

And then, out of nowhere, came a message. From her.

Christen Norris.

She had unblocked me.

For a second, I just stared at the screen. There was no preamble, no venom, no explanation—just a quiet little bomb of a message waiting for me to open it. And instead of panic, what I felt was a strange calm. Like some deeply buried instinct knew this would be important.

We had a messy history, she and I. Not from anything she had done—our bad blood had been artificially injected straight from the source: Jason. I'd been fed the usual script about the "jealous ex," the "crazy friend," "the dramatic nuisance who just couldn't let him go." And like so many women trying to believe their abuser, I'd swallowed it whole. We'd had one heated exchange back when I thought he was mine and she was just the unhinged warning light I refused to acknowledge. I didn't like her. I didn't trust her. I'd mentally written her off as unstable, because that's what he told me to believe.

But I also remembered, vaguely, a night when Jason was slurring his words and dropped a line that lodged itself somewhere in the back of my brain: "*You and Christen would probably get along*" and he wasn't wrong. *You know what they say about broken clocks.*

Her message said, "I got brave."

I blinked. Then typed back,

"You got brave?"

She responded that Jason was in jail. For beating her.

And without hesitation, my fingers moved on their own.

"He hit me too."

No warm-up. No carefully worded confession. Just the truth, raw and unfiltered, tumbling out like it had been waiting for permission to exist.

That was the moment the dam cracked. Not completely, but enough for light to get through. Enough for me to stop wondering if I'd imagined everything, or exaggerated, or brought it on myself. Because here was another woman, different from me in every way and yet cracked down the same middle, saying: *Me too.*

Christen, the girl I once saw as an enemy, became the first person who made me feel like I wasn't alone. Like maybe I wasn't overreacting. Like maybe what happened to me really did count. Her message didn't just give me clarity—it gave me company. And after six months in my own head, that was a lifeline I hadn't known I needed.

I didn't know yet how close we'd become, or how our stories would intertwine in the years ahead. But that night, something shifted. And thank God it did.

Chapter Four

The Cost of Silence

"I'm proud of who I am / No more monsters, I can breathe again." — Kesha, "Praying"

That first talk I had with my new friend was eye-opening, to say the least. It was jarring as hell. Christen bravely filled me in on her previous evening, and it was impossible not to want to reach through the phone and hug her. Each typed bubble felt like a punch to my gut, unraveling her harrowing tale bit by bit. She'd been found the night before by a Cleveland Police Officer, her face slick with blood, oozing from cuts Jason left on her skin. He'd savagely beaten her in his mother's driveway.

I'm not here to tell you Christen's story; I'd mess it up and not do her level of badassery justice. I do know this: Christen truly believed Jason was going to kill her that night. She also feared he'd end her for filling out her protective order. Turns out they were way more than just friends, and Jason's stack of lies was toppling over, one little blue text bubble at a time. Christen and Jason had struck up a relationship in July of 2013, becoming way more than just friends. Apparently, he'd straight-up proposed to her, and now he was out on bond for brutally attacking her in front of his mother's house—the little one with the Jesus statues and the varmints in the walls.

After Jason punched her in the nose twice, pulled her by the hair, smashed her face into the gravel, kicked her in the ribs, Christen began to scream and Jason managed to get ahold of her again. Slamming her head into the steering wheel of her car, honking the horn, realizing his mother Pam was in the house and would hear all of this commotion outside. She never came out.

Jason then fishhooked Christen, putting his fingers in her mouth, ripping her gumline from her cheek, and also bit her in the shoulder. Despite enduring all this torture, Christen had managed to get away, attempting to drive her black Dodge Charger to the police station, but ended up at Billy Vessels Park to calm her shaking hands and racing mind. Patrolling nearby was Cleveland Police Officer Russ Shouse.

Officer Shouse discovered Christen in her car that night, and unknowingly became a much-needed hero in this story. That single act may have saved her life—and it sure as shit changed mine. She was too scared to come forward on her own—Jason does that to a girl—but something about the stillness of that park gave her enough bravery to at least gather her wits. And Shouse, bless his uniform, had the decency to notice a woman in distress.

They offered Christen an ambulance, but she refused, though she did go to the Emergency Room in Tulsa the following day. Officer Shouse and a deputy officer arrested Jason within the hour.

Christen was able to obtain a Temporary Emergency Protective Order against Jason after her assault, describing what Jason had done to her. In her words, she wrote:

> *When Jason gets angry, he breaks things, and is physically violent to women. He, himself, has admitted this. He knows he has a problem. Last June, we went to Missouri on a weekend trip. He woke to find me looking through his cell phone, got angry, and spit in my face. Threatened to kill me, pushed me against the wall, ordered me to stay, pulled my hair. We were in a hotel room, it was around midnight, he made me pack up and take him back to Tulsa and wouldn't let me use my phone. And he pulled his gun out of the holster and laid it on his bag in the back seat. I drove him straight home. He threatened me and my children, and left.*

Last January, I met Jason and we went for a late-night drive. He was depressed about a custody case he was going through. He held a pistol to my head at my temple and under my chin, and when I started gasping and trying to catch my breath, he said, "That's what I feel like inside 24/7. I want you to know what it feels like." He eventually lowered the gun and we drove to his mom's house. He picked a fight with his mom when we arrived, broke mirrors, threw his phone and a vacuum. I left.

On March 21st, 2015, Jason sent me a message asking that I stop by on my way home from my sister's house in Fairfax. I got there, he got in the passenger's seat, he hit me in the arm and I told him to stop. He said it didn't hurt and slapped my face. I told him I didn't want to play like that. Then he smacked a cup in my face as I was taking a drink and it spilled down me. I got out of the car and came to the trunk to get a blanket to use to dry off. I shut the trunk, and went to the passenger's side, opened the door, and told Jason I would come and see him another day when he felt better. I told him I was going home.

He got mad and asked if I was kicking him out of my car. He grabbed the back of my head by my hair, spit in my face, and punched me in the face, still holding my hair. He took me over to the gravel rocks, pushed my chin to my chest, locking my head there by continuing to hold my hair as he pushed me down, face first into the gravel. I bit my tongue and had locked jaws but could not speak. I was pulled into an upright position and still holding my hair, he grabs my arm, pulls me near the driveway, and I broke loose. I ran to the neighbor's house and almost knocked.

I asked Jason if I could please just have my car and I would just leave. He told me to come closer, and if I didn't, it didn't matter because he could catch me in three steps. I came closer. He pulled me down on his lap in the passenger's seat while holding my head down with one arm. He was using his other arm to fishhook my mouth, separating my cheek from my gumline. I said, "Ouch, you're hurting me." He said, "That will teach you not to scream." He said, "Are you going to scream again?"

He let go of me and I made it to the street. He got out of the driver's seat and walked around to the passenger's side to find his phone. I got closer to the car; as he was shutting the passenger door, I locked myself in and quickly left. He threw full cans of beer at my car, and later sent me a text: "Funny how Sharon left a note on the door when you left. Just fucking jovial."

I went to the police station but wasn't sure if I was at the right place, and used that as an excuse to go think about everything that had just happened to me. While I was at the park, Officer Russ, of Cleveland PD, drove up and saw my face. He started asking questions. Russ asked me a few times if I would let him call an ambulance. I denied. I went to the hospital for treatment the next day. Jason is in jail and should be treated by a psychiatrist and completely rehabilitated before release. He has a history of violence against women. I am afraid he will kill me for writing this.

Christen had known of Jason since she was a kid. And I emphasize "of" because she never really knew him. If she had, she would've run like hell—and I wouldn't have this twisted, badass origin story of how I met my best friend.

Jason was in her class from kindergarten through high school, but they never spoke. She kept her distance, the way you instinctively steer clear of a stray dog foaming at the mouth. She remembered how he'd disappear for months at a time, only to hear he'd been "sent away" for behavior no one could seem to control. The rumors were always wild. Worse, they were often true.

I'll never forget her telling me how, in high school, he'd strut around like he owned the place—decked out in Guess jeans and designer shirts—even though his family didn't have a pot to piss in. Turns out, his dad, Jason Lewis Sr., had stolen an entire semi-truck full of Dillard's merchandise, and his mother sold it out of a shady knockoff storefront in Cleveland called Purple Rain. Eventually, the law caught up with Daddy Dearest and shipped him off to the state pen.

Runs in the family, I guess.

Christen had stories like this for days.

Skip ahead a decade or so to her brother's 40th birthday party. That's when Christen ran into Jason for the first time since those weird-ass high school days. He showed up with a girlfriend on his arm, all smiles and charm, playing the harmless card like a fucking pro. They struck up a friendship.

Let me pause here and properly introduce you to Christen. She's a goddamn force of nature. Blonde, tall, stunning in that *"bombshell meets girl-next-door with a plot twist"* kind of way. She looked like she belonged on the cover of *Architectural Digest* holding a glass of wine and a dog that doesn't shed. And funny? That woman could make you laugh so hard you'd cry into your Taco Bueno. She was sharp, magnetic, and completely unforgettable. Her birthday was exactly one week after mine, so naturally we bonded over being two Libra smart-asses trying to keep the peace while setting shit on fire. Our friendship was clearly helping us cope with just about everything life threw at us. My pinch hitter was doing some pretty heavy lifting, too.

Back to the story: Christen and Jason started hanging out more. Took trips out of town—just like he and I did later—and before long, he seduced the ever-loving shit out of her. At first, he played it cool. Sweet. Affectionate. Hooked her in with that fake charm. But like clockwork, the mask slipped. It always did.

Christen would later swear under oath that he held a gun to her face, screamed at her with spit flying, dragged her across gravel, fish-hooked her mouth until her gums tore, threatened her kids, and made her drive with him pointing a gun at her head. When I read those details, it felt like being kicked in the chest by a goddamn Clydesdale. I could hear the blood rushing in my ears. The monster that haunted my life had been ramping up—and she'd faced an even darker version of him. *I had been lucky.*

It broke my heart to hear her story. She was a successful realtor, a sharp, put-together single mom—exactly the kind of woman who should've had a damn security detail after what she endured. In all reality, Christen gave me my first shot of real, gut-deep validation. The shit he did to me wasn't isolated. *I wasn't crazy. And neither was she.*

Early on, she also told me about a story Jason once bragged about to her. According to him, back in the late '90s, he took some "crazy stripper" to Eureka Springs and she flipped out and called the cops on him. He told it like it was some wild weekend anecdote. We both knew deep down there was much more to the story about what happened that weekend in Arkansas.

But surely he hasn't been abusing without consequences since the nineties, I thought to myself.

Speaking of Eureka Springs—fall of 2014—Christen had lined up a whole weekend getaway with Jason. She rented the car, made the reservations, even booked a room at the famously haunted Crescent Hotel. It was supposed to be their thing. A little road trip romance, just like they'd planned. Only... he never showed. No call. No text. Nothing. Just *poof.* Gone. Like she didn't exist.

Meanwhile, I was in Branson, three and a half hours away, sitting across from him at a restaurant, totally oblivious. I didn't know he'd ghosted another woman like some emotionally bankrupt magician. I was playing tourist with a guy who had left someone else—someone kind and hopeful—burned and humiliated, holding the keys to a rental car and no fucking clue what happened.

He didn't just ditch her. He made her eat the cost and the confusion. She was stranded and blindsided. And me? I was on his arm thinking I was special.

But really, we were just different chapters in the same horror story.

But as sickening as it was to hear what he did to Christen that spring night in his mother's driveway, it turns out she wasn't the only woman Jason pounded into the ground that week. Sharon Lewis—the ex-wife he swore was obsessed with him—had also been absolutely brutalized. He choked her repeatedly, strangling her airway, and she explained in her report, "Because he used to be a mortician, he knows exactly the specific two places where to grab your throat to suffocate you the fastest." Not Sharon's first rodeo with him, either. Previous sworn statements said he'd spit in her face, drag her by the hair, bite her nose and ear, and pin her down so hard she pissed herself—telling her to "lay there and bleed out." One night, after beating her half to death, he dragged her to the bathroom and stood with her in front of the mirror to inspect her body for bruises. He intended to shoot her wherever she bruised because, in his fucked-up mind, he believed he could explain away the damage during an autopsy. Gentle reader, he made Sharon prep her own corpse for her own autopsy. That's the level of sickness we're dealing with.

Sharon's protective order from 2013 stated why she needed protection from Jason Lewis:

> *On the evening of May 13th, we got into an argument that led to him pulling my hair, throwing a heavy box at me, hitting me, and throwing me into the floor, and on the bed. He held his hand over my face, smashing my mouth and suffocating me, putting a split in my lip. After choking me and holding me down, he finally let me up. Cleaned the blood from my face and the pillow case and the bed. He then got on the phone and when he disappeared in the other room with the door closed, I grabbed a bag and clothes and ran to my car, leaving for approximately two hours. He and his mom both called my cell phone. I didn't answer his calls. But his mom said I should just stay in a hotel and not go home. I sent him a text message saying I just wanted to come home and go to bed. We haven't argued in a long time, and I thought he had time to cool off. When I got home, something was in front of the door, so I pushed hard, and pulled at the bottom of the hinge to get inside. He*

came running across the living room, grabbed me by my face and throat, calling me names, telling me not to come home. He threw me down in the living room floor by my hair, kicked me, jumped onto me, spit on me, choking me, drug me by my hair into the kitchen, kicked me and told me to go to our room. He threw me across the bed, I slid off the other side into some boxes and furniture. He jumped on top of me, crushing the air out of me, and hitting me in the head several times. He stayed on top of me, holding me down with force until I urinated on myself. He went to the bathroom and was smoking a cigarette, and I told him I couldn't breathe and asked for help. He told me to "lay there and bleed out." Then he pulled me onto the bed where he poked his finger into my right eye, choked me, and hit me in the head. After he calmed down for a moment, I went to the bathroom and I came back out and he told me to stop crying and he threw the remote control at me, hitting me in the forehead. Then he made me go back to the bathroom, he made me douche and cleaned from under my fingernails, he used bleach to clean the bathroom and told me how he was going to kill me. He lifted my shirt and bra, and pulled down my shorts looking for bruises. He told me he was going to shoot me to cover up the bruises, and explained how he could cover up anything that would be identified in an autopsy. Then he made me lay across our bed and told me he had two guns under his left hip and was waiting for me to go to sleep. He said he had a gun from someone that it wasn't registered to him and that it had a silencer on it. He went to my car and brought in all the things that I had taken out there and he laid next to me drinking beer and watching TV. He told me to set the alarm on his cell phone so I could go to work the next day and that if he ever heard me tell anyone about anything he would kill me. When the alarm went off, I ran to the car and left while he slept."

Sharon eventually confessed to us that Jason actually made her douche her vagina with liquid Clorox.

I learned after reading Sharon's protective order that Jason Lewis wasn't just an abuser. *He was a fucking monster.*

And to think, just months ago, I was running my smart mouth at him, clearly underestimating what he was capable of.

Sharon ended up waiting until April of 2015, almost a year later, to officially report these horrors to Sapulpa Police. She also filed a second protective order that day. She also reported a violation of that second protective order, but the police told her, "We haven't served him yet, so there can't be a violation, even though you have a protective order." As damning as Sharon's original accusations were, by the time court rolled around for her original Protective Order, Jason sweet-talked her (by threatening her) into dropping charges—he's that smooth, or maybe that evil. The Sapulpa Police and the Creek County District Attorney's Office just shrugged it off like he hadn't forced a woman to douche her vagina with cleaning chemicals. They treated her like the nutcase. Hell, even *I* assumed she might be a few crayons short of a full box; torture does that to a girl. Turns out physical and emotional abuse can warp the strongest mind, and Sharon was living proof.

Sharon's March 2015 protective order from an incident that happened in Bethany, Missouri in front of Jason's two young daughters. It stated:

> *I have suffered physical abuse from Jason for two years, off and on, he has promised to get help and stop abusing. He becomes violent and hostile, repeatedly lashing out. On March 14, of 2015, we were in a hotel in Bethany, MO with his two young daughters present. He began to drag me, pull my hair, choke me, and bang my head against the door. Called me vulgar names, cussed me, ordered me to the bathroom, and told me that I was traumatizing the girls because I wouldn't mind him. Once he had me in the bathroom, he proceeded to hold me by my hair, throw me down on the floor, ripped at my ears, and bit my face, he*

spit on me, and told me he would gouge my eyes out if he had to tell me twice to do what he says. My foot was injured from him stepping on me, and he pulled out hands full of hair. He told me to clean my face and fix my hair before I left the bathroom and was in front of his daughters. A few minutes later, there were two police officers at the door. Jason was confrontational and wouldn't let them in the room. One of them asked me to come out, and I did. I told him that we had a fight and that everything was okay now. I was afraid to have Jason arrested in front of the girls. The officer told me that they received a call that the kids were screaming for help and that someone was being beat up. I said I was okay, and then they left. Two days later I removed all of his personal belongings to a storage building, changed the locks at my house, and sent Jason a letter of eviction at his Mom's asking that he no longer come to my home. I'm afraid that he will come after me or my daughter. He has threatened her in revenge for my previous Protective Order, which he says costed him custody of his daughters in 2014. My children and I are very scared of him. He is scary and violent and seems to have some type of issue with anger and controlling his temper. He is also suicidal a large portion of the time. I am terrified he will kill me or possibly my kids before he hurts himself. He has said if he has nothing left to lose, he will take us all with him. I request that he be monitored if possible and that he be ordered to get help if possible. I also will call Sapulpa PD and request that an Officer will check up on my residence daily.

The Creek County District Attorney did not press charges.

After finding out he'd assaulted two women in one week, I felt this wave of guilt swallow me like a riptide. My chin quivered, my palms got clammy, and I tangled my fingers in my hair out of pure helpless anxiety. *I caused this.* By staying quiet, I let him run free to wreck more lives. *My silence enabled him. My mind screamed: Oh God, are there more?*

That night, my worldview snapped. I couldn't let little Karrah—farm kid Karrah—grow up to be the woman who just let monstrous men keep on terrorizing people. The urge to reach out to him swarmed over me. I wanted him to know that I knew what he did to those girls and somehow express the validation I was suddenly feeling. I sent him an email, toying with him, because I really just wanted to get a confession out of him. "I understand if you want to pay me $10,000 to stay quiet about what you did to me," I mischievously typed. I wanted him to know that I was about to 'out' him. *Was it stupid to throw a bribe in there?* Of course, but I knew there was no way in hell he was ever going to give me any kind of money.

I just wanted him to confess to what he did to me. He outsmarted me that day, and I did not get the confession I was hoping for. It wasn't something I was proud of, but looking back, I understand what was going through my mind. I was trying to outsmart a master manipulator when I am not one.

Sending him a shitty email was obviously not enough. I had to do something huge. The idea of him threatening my daughter again made me want to vomit, but I clung to the hope the police would protect us. After all, *I've never filed a police report, I'm from a decent family, I have a steady job—don't I deserve at least minimal safety here?* Then there was the other roadblock: if I told the cops, I'd also be confessing to the world that I was a domestic violence victim. *Gross.* That label is suffocating, and it's laced with shame. But the reality? *My fear was fueling his freedom.* More women would take that beating if I didn't step up.

So yeah, bring on the shame. If it meant he couldn't keep racking up new victims, I'd deal with it.

I knew I had to tell the police what he did to me.

Both Christen and Sharon were just beginning their own legal hell with him by the time we met. They each had to fight for protective orders after escaping his violence—fighting for something that should've been automatic, but instead felt like begging. And of course, in true Jason fashion, he tried to flip the script and filed retaliatory protective orders against both of them. He served Christen at work, deliberately trying to humiliate her in front of her co-workers. When Christen tried to have him served, he actually told the process server his name was "Todd," because apparently, that was the best plan his tiny brain could come up with to temporarily dodge accountability. Sharon faced the same exhausting circus. She was forced into courtrooms to defend herself against his retaliatory protective order, which was ultimately denied—but not before she had to stand there while he weaponized the system to drag her through it all over again.

And as if that weren't enough, during one of Christen's protective order hearings, they made her sit directly across from him—her first time seeing him since escaping his abuse. He sat close enough to practically touch her, legs spread wide like he was claiming territory. She could smell his breath. His smugness filled the entire goddamn room. That's what the Oklahoma justice system called protection.

Sharon and I were there to support Christen that day. And that's when I saw him up close for the first time since that night on the highway when he clocked me across the face. We were leaving court when I ran into him in a dim, musty stairwell. There was no distance this time. No gallery seats to separate us. Just the two of us, face to face, in that tight space.

My heart was doing wind sprints in my chest, but I refused to back down. I squared my shoulders, glared, and from some deep-rooted bravado, I said firmly, "Fuck you."

He stammered back, "F-f-fuck you!" like he'd just flunked a tough-guy audition. I let a slow grin curl across my face—pure rebel theatrics. He wasn't expecting that. Inside, though, *I was shaking like a chihuahua that thinks it's a Rottweiler.* That moment captured everything: outwardly, I was the badass telling him to go to hell; inwardly, *I was counting the seconds until I could breathe normally again.* It was the showdown I never wanted but couldn't dodge—so I stood my ground, shaky legs and all.

Fuck, that felt good.

Chapter Five

The Unicorn Club

"You don't take shit and you don't settle / You don't play dumb and you don't backpedal." — K.Flay, "Sister"

Filing that first police report was terrifying, mostly because I'd spent my entire life not expecting to need one. Yet there I was, walking into the Sapulpa Police Station with shaky hands, bracing myself to spill the ugliest secrets of my short but brutal relationship with Jason Lewis. I'd always imagined some big dramatic moment where an officer would hand me tissues and promise, "We'll bring him in right away, ma'am." Spoiler alert: that did not happen.

At least I didn't go alone. Christen—bless her heart—insisted on coming with me so I wouldn't have to face it by myself. She understood the fear, the shame, and the sick feeling in your stomach when you finally say the words out loud. Just having her there made it feel a little less impossible.

Author's Note:

I'm about to share my official police report exactly as I wrote it in my shaky handwriting all those years ago. I didn't want to. Honestly, I thought the worst details of that night would stay locked in the deepest part of my brain forever, but apparently, trauma doesn't play by the rules. As I'm writing this book, I've done my best to lay out everything I genuinely remember happening. But as I re-read the words I wrote on that police report, I realized with a sickening feeling in my stomach that there were things I described clearly then that my brain has completely blocked out now. It's bizarre and unsettling—like reading someone else's horrible memories. That's the thing about trauma—it doesn't always come in loud and obvious. Sometimes it hides in the dark corners of your brain, too unbearable to carry front and center. It's kind of like childbirth. If women actually remembered every god-awful second of it in vivid detail, we'd have had a serious population problem a long time ago. But the brain steps in, does a little erasing, a little softening—because survival depends on it. Trauma works the same way. My mind pulled the emergency brake, blacked out the stuff it couldn't handle, and filed it under do not disturb. It tried its ass off to protect me. So, when you read the following police report, please know these aren't fresh memories. They're words from a younger, frightened me who was desperately trying to document the horrors clearly enough to get justice—even if today, I don't fully remember living through some of them. Consider this a gentle heads-up: what you're about to read is exactly what I wrote down for the police, even though my brain did its best to delete it.

This is what I wrote in my messy left-handed handwriting when the memories were still very fresh:

"I met Jason Lewis and thought I had found Mr. Right. He took me to Branson on our first date. Looking back, that was the first time he hit me. I was drying my hair and was hit by a belt. When I cried from hurting, he told me I was crazy. Several incidents happened over a month, but in Sapulpa City Limits he punched me in the face as I was driving down the road, pulled my hair, played with my eyeballs, slammed my head on my car window. He forced me to have anal sex with him until my rectum was torn. Over a 5-hour period. Forced me to use a dildo that

> *I didn't want inside of me. For hours. Held my hair and slammed it on the shower. Held me against my will while he beat me and slammed my head on the window. Forced a bottle in my vagina when I was sleeping (I didn't have the nerve to say it was my ass for some reason). Threw a chair at me, punched a hole in the wall, and choked me instead of hitting me, and said I was 'lucky.' Choked me until I passed out two different times. Choked me multiple times. Told me he would kill my daughter if I told the police."*

The minute I finished recounting how he beat me, fishhooked my damn mouth, threatened my daughter's life, and forced me to do his twisted bidding, I braced for sirens. For a knock on his door. For justice. Instead, I got a polite nod, a half-hearted "We'll look into it," and the heart-sinking realization that Jason would probably waltz around free as a pigeon, feathers unruffled. They didn't even bring him in for questioning. Not once. Not even to hear his version of events. Because the minute he got wind that I had spoken up, he lawyered up and refused to cooperate with Detective Amy Nichols, the "public servant" who was assigned my case. And just like that, her investigation stalled out. Probably no further questions, probably no follow-up. They let him hide behind a lawyer while I walked around raw and exposed.

I couldn't even get a goddamn protective order against the man who threatened to murder my child. Christen and Sharon had their little pieces of paper stamped by a judge. I didn't even have that. No safety net. No legal shield. Just the hollow promise of a system that looked me in the eye and decided I wasn't worth the paperwork. My jugular felt exposed.

Filing my first police report of my life wasn't a total dead end, however. The Sapulpa Police did put me in touch with Domestic Violence Intervention Services (DVIS). That's how I ended up filling out a rape intake form, which felt surreal—like I was in some alternate universe. Even though I'd already connected with Christen and Sharon over the shared nightmare of Jason's abuse, group therapy at DVIS was where we all gathered together in the same physical space—free to compare every bruise and heartbreak under the watchful eye of our therapist, Cynthia.

Cynthia was the one who kept drilling it into our heads: *"This is not your fault. Jason is a predator—nobody's immune to a conman."* Hearing that was like being handed a life raft after treading water for far too long. She broke down Jason's narcissistic bullshit with the nuance of a UFC commentator: first the love bombing, then devaluation, discard, and another round of love bombing until you either get wise or die. The more she explained, the more every broken part in my brain began to click into place like a puzzle I never wanted to own in the first place.

*

But through all that bullshit—the court dates, the gaslighting, the "how-is-this-still-legal" level of injustice—the Unicorn Club became our shelter, our war room, and our sanctuary. We weren't just survivors trading horror stories over coffee. We were sisters-in-arms, each of us holding a piece of the same shattered mirror, finally seeing the full reflection of what we'd been through.

We had each other's backs like bodyguards in a courtroom full of snakes. We'd sit on those stiff-ass benches, watching him pull the same cowardly moves over and over again—postponements, continuations, smug grins—and we'd give each other the kind of side-eyes that said, *This motherfucker again?*

Christen even offered Sharon a chance to partner with her in her cleaning business—one Christen had already built and grown for years. It was her way of extending not just friendship, but opportunity, a way for Sharon to rebuild and move forward.

And yeah, we went on a cruise to Mexico. Just three traumatized badasses in flip-flops, chasing tequila with belly laughs and reclaiming joy in the most rebellious way we knew how: by refusing to stay small.

Laughter helped. A lot. So did calling his dick a *"tater tot,"* which became a running joke and a tiny form of vengeance that lived rent-free in our group chat. And we didn't even come up with it—Jason did. He actually referred to his own dick as a tater tot to each of us, like some twisted fishing expedition, hoping we'd lie and say, *"No, Jason , you're totally hung like a gorilla."* But what helped most wasn't the jokes. It was the sacred, electric truth of it all: *we weren't crazy. We weren't overreacting. And we sure as hell weren't alone.*

We were the Unicorn Club—rarer than rare, stronger than trauma, and loud enough to be dangerous.

So that's when our little warrior collective we called the Unicorn Club was born—though it started as more of a joke between bruised women who'd endured the same demon. It didn't take long to morph into a true alliance. We realized we'd all been fish-hooked by his thumb, had guns pointed at us, threatened with kidnapping, dragged to random rural spots like Frog Rock, Sandy Point, and Boston Pool Road. And dear God, Jason's "Are you my unicorn?" line was apparently a standard reel he used on each of us. Nothing like discovering your personal romantic hell was plagiarized and passed around to other victims, too.

I also learned I wasn't his only conquest that involved a weird private showing of the movie *Divergent*. As it turns out, in October

2014, the same week he carted me to the video store for that movie, he took two more women there and forced them to watch the same flick at his place. I still have no clue why *Divergent* was so special—maybe he just liked seeing strong female leads get manipulated by authoritarian weirdos? *Now there's irony for you.* Or maybe he just wanted to impress the video store clerk.

And let's not forget Sharon. She'd definitely been with him the longest and had the worst stories—he forced her to urinate on herself, made her douche with bleach, and threatened to shoot her in the bruises he left. He basically battered her psyche until she lived for his lame apologies. Meanwhile, Christen was still reeling from the time he held a gun to her head, forcing her to drive at gunpoint while he spat in her face. And me? I clocked in at just three weeks, but that was enough for him slam his fist into my face and degrade me in ways I won't unfeel anytime soon.

Yet somehow, we laughed when we were together. We discovered that so many of his big claims—his personal assistant "Vicki," the pilot's license, the plane, the law degree—were total scams. The day Christen found out Vicki Brochan was actually Jason catfishing as a Russian bride-level hottie, we lost our collective shit. He had an entire side gig as a fake sexy lady to help promote his business ventures, and men online fawned over "her." Our battered souls needed that comedic relief. Even though picturing him in some half-assed push-up bra gave me the creeps, it also made him look damn pathetic.

His beautiful house wasn't even his. He was renting it from a lady named Donna Walkingstick, who ended up evicting him, complaining of damage to the house, including the shattered glass oven door he was kind enough to break on our second date. The same glass Christen swept up for him the morning after my night from hell. Turns out, his house was a revolving glass door of unicorns.

Funnily enough, I found out Jason was showing pictures of my professionally carved pumpkins to women and telling them he created them. *Who pretends to be a professional pumpkin carver? It's weird enough actually being one.*

Lastly, I have not confirmed with country singer Sara Evans if she has a child with Jason Lewis, but something tells me she will not be suing him for child support any time soon.

The Unicorn Club didn't remain exclusive for long. The more we talked, the more other women came forward with the same story: Jason Lewis is a monster. After channeling our best *Cagney & Lacey*, we found out Jason's rap sheet of Emergency Protective Orders stretched back to 1998. One was permanent, meaning a judge physically wrote something with the sentiment, *Stay the hell away from this woman forever.* That poor lady was a University of Tulsa law student—he nearly destroyed her. She vanished out of Oklahoma, refusing to be found. We also discovered that he had actually badly beaten the young girl in Eureka Springs, Arkansas in 1997, and that he'd also beaten Maggie, the ex-wife he was fighting for custody.

Sharon was his third marriage by then. The deeper we dug, the more we realized we were just a few among a long line of battered women Jason had terrorized.

A rare ray of sunshine finally peeked through this absolute shitstorm when Christen managed to shove her assault case into the Pawnee County courts. Jason was being charged with Assault & Battery for what he did to Christen. She was determined to hold him accountable for beating the hell out of her in his mom's driveway, but true to form, the system responded with a gigantic middle finger.

The Sunday evening before she was due in court—after mentally preparing herself to face him—Christen got a casual phone call from the Pawnee County DA's office: "You don't need to come tomorrow, it's been rescheduled." Trusting the system (rookie mistake), Christen stayed home. And while she wasn't there, Jason and his slimy-ass attorney slid in and cut a backdoor deal with the Assistant DA. Jason walked out with 18 months of unsupervised probation—basically a *try not to beat anyone else or we'll act mildly disappointed* sentence—and a laughable 52 weeks of online Anger Management. Because apparently, you can cure being a violent psychopath by clicking through PowerPoint slides in your pajamas.

In real-world terms, unless Jason knocked the teeth out of yet another woman, he wouldn't spend any real time behind bars. He got credit for time already served and avoided any meaningful jail sentence. Christen was livid. And to me, it felt like taking another beer bottle to my asshole. Once again, he walked out free—stalking, terrorizing, threatening—while the Pawnee County court system shrugged like, *Eh, maybe we'll care once he finally kills somebody.*

But Christen wasn't done. She channeled every ounce of that rage into action. First, she filed a civil lawsuit against Jason and his enabler of a mother, Pam, for negligence. She went straight for Pam's home-owner's insurance. The woman who sat quietly in her house while Jason turned her driveway into his personal fight club finally had to face something resembling consequences. The case eventually settled out of court. It wasn't justice, but it was at least a small, satisfying *fuck you.*

And still, Christen kept pushing. She took the transcripts from Jason's criminal plea—where he admitted guilt—and marched herself right into the sheriff's office and the DA's office. She asked the question any halfway competent prosecutor should've asked already: *How can this man admit guilt and then sit in that exact same court-room and deny ever laying a hand on me?* She had the proof in black and white. For a moment, it looked like the system might finally get it right. The DA promised to file felony perjury charges. We even let ourselves imagine the perp walk.

Instead? They let him do a walkthrough booking like it was a damn dental appointment. And then quietly dropped the charges altogether. Just like that. Gone. Another escape hatch.

And still, Christen had to fight like hell for every tiny scrap of accountability. Oklahoma never cared. But she never stopped.

By May 2015, I felt sure the cops weren't going to handle this. So when the Assistant District Attorney of Creek County, Laura Farris, agreed to meet with me, Christen, and Sharon, we jumped at the chance like it was the last lifeboat on the Titanic. For a few seconds there, I had hope that my case wasn't dead in the water. That maybe, just maybe, something would finally happen. I had hope that he was going to be prosecuted for torturing Sharon.

We spent an hour and twenty-six minutes in her office on the top floor of the Creek County Courthouse, unloading everything: the bleach douches, the fists to the face, the gun threats, the manipulated retaliation protective orders. Every horrifying detail, laid bare. I recorded that meeting because at this point, *fuck it.* I was surprisingly quiet that day, still choking on the memory of what he'd done to me. When Laura asked me point-blank, "What did Jason do to you?" I wanted to scream *He beat and raped me,* but the words got stuck.

The best I managed was, *"He hurt me."* That's still humiliating as hell to recall.

When we finally stopped talking, she sat there, nodding, taking notes, acting like she might actually do something with all of it. And then she let us down easily. She said she would look into our cases, but without video evidence or hard proof, there wasn't much she could promise. In fact, she gently suggested that if we were still worried for our safety, we should consider buying deer cams to monitor our homes. This was before Ring doorbells had really taken off and gotten cheap enough for regular people to afford. So yeah—deer cams. That was their advice.

It was just another time the system dangled hope in front of us, only to yank it away. Another *almost.* Another *nothing.*

Going to group therapy with Christen and Sharon gave me the courage to not freak out when I met someone new. His name was Chad. Tall, good-looking, strong, with just enough soft around the edges to make me feel... safe. He worked hard. He was kind. A genuinely good man, which felt like spotting a goddamn endangered species at that point in my life. I wasn't ready. Not really. But I wanted to be. I was still tangled in trauma, still waking up in cold sweats, still scanning every room for exits. But Chad was patient, and that first night we finally slept together, I surprised myself—I didn't freeze up. I didn't dissociate. I didn't feel dirty or ruined. I felt okay.

Almost human again.

Until the next morning.

He stood up to go to the bathroom, and that's when I saw it—a tattoo on his back. I don't even remember what it was. All I could see were two Roman columns.

And just like that, my nervous system took over, and I wasn't in Chad's bed anymore—I was back in Jason's evolving torture chamber of a bedroom, staring at the same symbol I'd memorized in fear. The oversized "II" from his back. My brain screamed, my body followed. I pissed myself. Right there on his bed. Soaked the sheets belonging to a perfectly decent man who hadn't done a damn thing wrong—except exist in a body that accidentally triggered mine.

Chad didn't get mad. He was compassionate. But I knew—I was nowhere near ready. PTSD doesn't care how sweet someone is. It only cares about what it remembers.

After that day, back tattoos stopped scaring me. *Who knew healing looked like an unexpected piss puddle on a good man's bed?* Small price for progress.

Unfortunately, my PTSD reared its ugly head more than once during our short time together, and I wasn't ready to let someone else carry that weight. I spared Chad the burden of helping me heal, and we only lasted a few months.

After hearing nothing for almost a year, I called the detective handling my case to check on its status. The Sapulpa Detective gently informed me they'd dropped my case against Jason without even bringing him in for questioning. "It's your word against his," she explained. "Bring it, then," I said. "Give me a jury, any jury." My pleas to her did not work. The man beat at least four women in his house in Sapulpa during the fall of 2014 in their county, but there was nothing they could do about it. *Right on cue, my frustration soared.*

Barely a week after that, my mom lost her battle with Early Onset Alzheimer's Disease.

Chapter Six

Wildfire

"And the pony she named 'Wildfire' busted down its stall." —Michael Martin Murphey, "Wildfire"

My mother's death should've broken me completely, but instead, it lit an angry fire under my ass. She was a fighter—she would've wanted me to keep going. So Christen and I hatched a plan: if the system wouldn't warn women about Jason, we would. And thus, we marched forward, hearts pounding, middle fingers raised, refusing to let that tater-tot-dicked psychopath keep racking up new victims. If the police weren't going to warn his next survivor, we were sure going to try. *Go big or go home.*

Christen had already compiled a comprehensive Word document chronicling the disturbing timeline of cruelty left behind by Jason Lewis, so it didn't take me long to turn that document into a full-fledged high-res color flyer. Armed with my graphic art skills and

Adobe InDesign (which I routinely use for designing publications for major corporations), I began to create the ugliest piece of work I had—or ever will—create. But it had to be done. By then, it wasn't difficult to find a good, recent mugshot of his sorry face. I slapped his ugly mug on that poster with a smile on my face, feeling a jolt of adrenaline I hadn't felt in months. If the system won't stop him, maybe we can at least rattle his cage.

Given my professional experience, crafting the flyer was a breeze—took me less than 15 minutes. I poured my heart and soul into it, making sure every detail of Christen's spreadsheet was highlighted, and adding a few extra accusations I'd uncovered.

It started with a big bold headline above his mugshot in red letters:

"WARNING:"

Then in big bold black letters: "SERIAL ABUSER AT LARGE IN YOUR NEIGHBORHOOD."

The flyer featured a comprehensive list of documented charges and accusations against Jason Lewis, leaving no room for doubt regarding his depravity.

The current accusations at the time were:

- Assault/Battery
- Rape
- Biting

- Spitting
- Choking
- Slapping
- Fish Hooking
- Held Hostage at Gunpoint
- Sodomy
- Threatening Lives of Children
- Stalking
- Conspiracy
- Kidnapping
- Felony Perjury
- Gross Negligence

I included his past and current case numbers, which were (big surprise) scattered across multiple states. I included the mystery case from Arkansas we had learned about, as well as various court dealings in Oklahoma (including a lawsuit involving caskets, because why not?). I also added pictures of the eight total victims we'd identified, a jarring visual to show people exactly how many lives he'd tried to ruin. I tried to hide the women's identities by placing large black bars over their eyes, although, in hindsight, I wished I hadn't used their faces at all. But at the time, I needed strangers to feel the impact of his warpath—that domestic violence could happen to anyone—and to see we were real humans, not invisible statistics. We had:

1. Survivor #1 – Mindy (OK): (A beautiful Native American single mom, briefly dated Jason—confided to a friend that he was violent and she lived in daily fear.)

2. Survivor #2 – Maggie, Wife #2 (OK): (Lived with his abuse for years, eventually divorced him and moved her two children to Iowa.)

3. Survivor #3 – Keely (OK): (Dated Jason briefly. He was extremely violent, but she didn't report it. Instead, she had a group of badass bikers escort him off her property.)

4. Survivor #4 – Sharon, Wife #3 (OK): (Brutalized sexually and physically by Jason. She reached out to authorities, but charges never materialized—even though he was literally *having* her prep her own body for an autopsy.)

5. Survivor #5 – Christen (OK): (Savagely attacked in his mother's driveway, resulting in an Assault & Battery charge that led nowhere. No real jail time.)

6. Survivor #6 – Karrah (Me, OK): (Beaten and raped—my own personal horror story.)

7. Survivor #7 – Brittany: (Dated Jason on and off, badly beaten by him.)

8. Survivor #8 – Cassidy (TU Law, late '90s): (Awarded a permanent protective order against him.)

I also included the lines: "TOTAL JAIL TIME SERVED: 2 DAYS"

And right under that: "FINAL PROTECTIVE ORDERS: 4"

I also included the statistic: "The Center for Disease Control's National Violence Against Women Survey found that the lifetime prevalence of rape, physical violence, and/or stalking toward women by an intimate partner to be greater in Oklahoma than any other state."

I ended it with the hashtag #TillItHappensToYou, pulled straight from the gut-wrenching Lady Gaga song she wrote about her own sexual assault. It felt like the perfect battle cry—raw, personal, undeniable. And yeah, maybe deep down I secretly hoped Mother Monster herself would catch wind of the story. If anyone understood the power of using your voice when the world tells you to shut up, it was her.

A few days after my mom's funeral, I had hit my fucking limit. Grief laid the kindling and Christen kindly handed me a match. I had reached the end of my rope—and Christen was right there, already gripping hers. My mom died on March 6, 2016, and while I was still drowning in grief, something inside me snapped—but not in a breakdown kind of way. *More like a fuck-around-and-find-out kind of way.* I'd been mourning one of the toughest women I've ever known, and somewhere in that grief, I found a grit I never knew I had in me. If the cops wouldn't step up and stop him from hurting more women, we'd make damn sure someone did.

So we made a plan. Nothing fancy, just two pissed-off women with a printer and enough righteous wrath to fuel a coup. The next day, we'd run off a couple hundred copies of my freshly designed fuck-off manifesto to Jason Lewis and paper every flat surface in his hometown with the truth. Cleveland, Oklahoma was about to get its first unsolicited truth drop.

It wasn't just rebellion and desperation—it was war. And my chest wasn't tight with nerves anymore, it was pounding with purpose. Our pain had turned into rocket fuel. The world had looked the other way long enough. *We weren't asking anymore.* I barely slept that night, buzzing like a kid before Christmas—if Santa were delivering vengeance and office supplies.

🔥

I woke up the next morning—D-Day, if you will—fully expecting Christen to have changed her mind. I felt my stomach clench thinking, *I can't do this alone.* But she was ready to rock and roll, and I felt a surge of relief. We were pumped to expose the rapist who threatened our kids' lives. Christen's real estate office became our temporary situation room as we quietly printed several hundred color copies of the flyer, definitely abusing her office copy machine policy (sorry, color ink is fucking expensive). After nearly getting busted by one of her coworkers, I noticed every single flyer we printed had my email address at the bottom. I tore it off of each copy—no way was I leaving my name for him to see, even if he likely guessed it was me.

For this mission, we needed to stay incognito. Neither of us wanted this bully's wrath at our doorstep. After stocking our "go bag" of flyers like we were offering a pizza sale, we swung by Tulsa International Airport and rented a car—a white Ford Mustang that wouldn't trace back to either of us.

Christen and I had a fast-burning tradition of belting out our favorite '80s country ballads anytime we were in a car together. She's actually got a lovely voice—clear, strong, always on key. I, however, sound like a raccoon doing karaoke in a rusty trash can. But that never stopped me. We sang loud and proud.

The name *Wildfire* came to us fast. We were driving a Mustang on a mission, and somewhere in our mental jukebox, that old Michael

Martin Murphey song kicked in: *"And the pony she named Wildfire..."*

My momma loved that song.

Between the mission, the Mustang, and those cheesy lyrics, the name just fit. *Wildfire* was the perfect name for our protest pony.

And once we named her, it became our rally cry:

"We shall spread the truth like Wildfire."

She wasn't just a car. She was our anthem. Our momentum. Our four-wheeled middle finger to the system that kept looking the other way.

Yes, we were very corny, but we were desperately determined to spread the truth like flames devouring a dry forest. I pulled a black hoodie over my head, jammed a baseball cap low, threw on sunglasses, and tried to steady my breathing. I was the good kind of nervous, partly from fear and partly from fuck-this-guy adrenaline as we peeled onto the highway toward Pawnee County.

Our journey through Cleveland was a rush—a Bonnie & Clyde spree armed with nothing but Scotch tape, thumbtacks, and my ugly masterpiece. My heart hammered every time we pulled into a parking lot, scanning for onlookers like we were in some heist movie. We plastered flyers on the corkboard at Jason's favorite restaurant (right next to the homemade signs for lawn mowing, free kittens, and fresh eggs for sale), the library door (right next to the book drop), the Police Station, the High School, Wal-Mart, the local feed store. Each time, Christen pulled up close, I bolted out of the late model Ford Mustang, slapped up a flyer, and lunged back into the car, seatbelt clicking with a shaky *Go! Go! Go!* Looking back on that day, I wish some camera had caught us so I could watch this insane moment of vigilante justice from a safe distance.

The whole day felt like we were starring in some offbeat indie film—two pissed-off women on a vigilante road trip, armed with flyers instead of guns. I kept catching myself thinking, *Damn, this is the kind of shit you see in movies,* except most of those are fiction. But here we were, living it for real, sweaty palms and all. I couldn't shake the feeling that one day someone might actually play us in a based-on-a-true-story film, and we were very much in the middle of that story, writing the script in real time. It was surreal and thrilling and scary as hell, like the universe had clicked on its overhead projector and said, *Lights, camera, go fuck him up.* And we did. *Manifestation, or whatever.*

By early evening on March 19, 2016, after hanging our flyer all over Boston Pool Road, we ended up at the municipal golf course perched on a hill just south of town to watch the sunset. My pulse still throbbed in my ears as we gazed at the setting sun. *Fact was, we still needed to do something with the remaining stack of flyers on the dashboard.* Cleveland is a small town, and we ran out of surfaces to cover, so we had quite a few leftover pieces. It was then, even though we're both total tree-huggers, we each clasped about half of the remaining stack of flyers and on the count of three, we tossed them into the wind. *Fuck it.* We wanted these seeds of truth to scatter across Cleveland, Oklahoma so that his neighbors, friends, and random bystanders would know exactly the kind of monster roaming their streets.

Our mission carried a simple motto: "The truth shall be spread like Wildfire." And on that day, as we flung those pages into the fading light, I felt a twisted sense of victory and terror all at once. Maybe we'd be pissing Jason off. Maybe we'd be risking more violence. But Goddamn it, at least we were doing something—dragging his secrets into the daylight so justice, or the nearest angry vigilante, might finally step in. We could lay our heads down that night knowing we had done our part to warn his future victims.

We had exposed a monster.

Chapter Seven

The Aftershock

"Put on your war paint." — Fall Out Boy, "The Phoenix"

The full-body high of sticking it to that violent son of a bitch didn't last. For a second, I felt like I'd just yanked the fire alarm in hell—loud, bold, and maybe even heroic. But reality? She shows up like a hangover. Loud. Miserable. Unforgiving.

I hadn't really thought it through—not all the way. I was so wrapped up in the adrenaline rush of finally doing something—of refusing to stay silent—that I didn't stop to consider what might come next. So when Jason Lewis came unglued and started threatening to sue every woman featured on the flyer, it hit like a slap I should've seen coming. He launched into a thermonuclear freakout, firing off threats like a man desperate to reassert control. And honestly? *I'd handed him the damn cigarette lighter.*

Christen, meanwhile, was already in her own legal minefield with him. The judge barely saw her as credible to begin with—already halfway convinced she was the unstable one in that three-ring circus. She couldn't come forward and admit she was the one driving the Mustang that day, even though she was. Even though it was the truth. Because in court, optics matter the most. And my impulsive, hot-blooded move had just put someone I loved in a dangerous position. *That's a weight I still carry.*

As if the fear of an impending lawsuit wasn't enough, Jason had already fired off a barrage of emails to my employers—yes, plural—painting me as a "drug-addicted harm to small children." His words, not mine. It was some next-level bullshit. I'd recently left Saied Music Company because I couldn't fake my bubbly *"Let's learn class piano!"* personality while standing up to a bully and healing bruises. Instead, I started teaching private lessons at a small studio near home—owned by my daughter's elementary school principal and dear friend—and picked up a part-time gig designing apartment maps for a small design firm.

Turns out Jason didn't think I needed to have a job. The worst part? He sent that smear campaign before we even papered his hometown with the flyers. It's like he saw it coming—like he knew I'd eventually get brave, and this was his preemptive strike. *If I'd known that little tidbit, I might've slapped a neon banner across every flyer that read, "Also, he's already trying to ruin my livelihood. Thanks for coming to my TED Talk."*

Thankfully, Roger Johnson—the owner of Overedukated, where I was teaching piano five nights a week—mostly saw through the bullshit. *Mostly.* He'd known me for years since he was the principal at my daughter's Elementary School. But when Jason messaged the studio accusing me of being a drug addict, Roger gave me the gist of Jason's accusations but kindly asked me not to involve the studio in my "personal problems." *(Which was sweet, really—like I'd requested a smear campaign.)*

When I told him I was trying to hold Jason accountable for hurting me and others, he said, "Maybe you should let it go."

That familiar line always stung, and it seemed the ones that loved me the most were the best at saying it. Roger wouldn't even show me the messages.

But I wasn't about to let it slide. I knew this could be grounds for a protective order. So I walked next door to the art studio and found Donna—the wildly talented art teacher Roger had hired, who also taught for Sapulpa Public Schools. Without missing a beat, she logged into the studio's Facebook page and printed Jason's lies off for me right then and there. Calm, steady, and all heart—Donna showed me in thirty seconds that she was truly a badass and an ally in a paint-splattered apron.

The design job? They never even told me Jason had reached out. I didn't find out until months later. *I guess they liked my map drawings enough not to care whether or not I was a drug addict.*

One of Jason's messages read:

"Having Karrah employed at your facility, ESPECIALLY being near young children, is a tremendous mistake on your part. There are a multitude of individuals throughout this area who will advise you of the same. I would further suspect if they are made aware that she is working with children at your facility, they would voice this on your wall and reflect your judgment of employees on your rating. Simply making you aware. —Jason"

Cute, right?

Luckily, I kept both jobs, and my student-count continued to grow. The parents of my students defended me feverishly. But between the sabotage, the threats, and even some survivors starting to turn on me, I was spinning in an EF5 tornado of *What the actual fuck is happening?*

By the time I had swallowed down my final dose of, *"Maybe you should move on,"* I was done waiting for the next grenade to go off. Jason had officially crossed into DEFCON Crazy, accusing me of being a danger to kids, a drug addict, and—his favorite recurring insult—a woman who cries rape every time she gets dumped by someone. *(Newsflash: I have never accused anyone of rape other than Jason Lewis.)* But this time, he didn't just post it for his 15 loyal Facebook followers. He put it in writing and sent it to people who signed my paychecks.

It was defamatory. It was dangerous. And it was the final straw.

For the first time, I had something real: a credible witness. Roger Johnson had seen the message firsthand, and he didn't hesitate to say it was bullshit. That made him more than a friend—he was leverage. So I marched into the courthouse, rattled but ready, and filed for an emergency protective order. Not because I thought it would stop Jason. *Please.* But because I was done showing up to this war unarmed.

I laid it all out—every threat, every harassment attempt, the smear campaign in full Technicolor. And when I signed that form, I wasn't scared.

I was pissed.

I was, however, granted a Temporary Emergency Protective Order that day, and was looking forward to the scheduled hearing to see if it would become permanent. Not permanent like the TU Law Student's. Hers was forever. In Creek County, "Permanent" meant one year. But I would have settled for a week of feeling safe by that point.

When it came to the flyer, it didn't take long to realize I'd have to be the one to take the hit. Someone had to absorb the full force of Jason's legal tantrum, and like an idiot with her arms wide open, I volunteered as tribute. Not because I was fearless—but because I couldn't stomach the idea of these other women, already chewed up and spit out by him, being dragged back into his cruel little world.

Even if it felt like I was being tossed under a fleet of Greyhound buses. In traffic.

On March 24th—just five days after Christen and I went full *Thelma and Louise*—I hit "Post" on Facebook and let the flyer digitally fly. And in a moment of what I can only call wishful thinking wrapped in cowardice, I claimed it had been created by *"a group of domestic violence advocates."*

Technically? Not a lie.

Realistically? A little duct tape over a bullet wound.

That little white lie didn't hold.

Jason was already threatening to sue every woman featured on the flyer—except the one with the forever protective order, and I think even he knew better than to test those waters. The rest? He went after them one by one, and I watched in horror as the solidarity we'd built started to unravel.

They were scared. I get it. But suddenly, I was the problem. The reckless one. The troublemaker. The one who made everything worse.

And so—with a lump in my throat and my stomach in knots—I stepped into the damn crosshairs. Not as some noble act of martyrdom, but because I didn't want his other survivors turning on me. Because I couldn't bear to have them hate me for trying to help.

I didn't think it through. Not really.

And Jason? He played it perfectly.

He framed me as the villain in the story I was trying to end. Told anyone who would listen that I made the flyers because I couldn't stand not having him back. That I was some jealous, crazy ex—scorned for not being his one-horned mythical creature.

He said I was just bitter about his new girlfriend, so I made up a bunch of lies about him.

And for a while... his story worked.

Then came April 1, 2016—April Fools' Day, which felt about right—when I opened my mailbox and found the punchline: a civil defamation lawsuit. The man who beat and raped me was now suing me for Civil Defamation and monetary damages that would later be determined. Jason was telling people he was going for $300,000.

A lawsuit that threatened to silence me and financially wreck me for years. Three hundred thousand dollars. From a man who should've been behind bars, not behind a legal filing.

And sure, I had no intention of ever shutting up or paying him a dime—I would've moved to Mexico and changed my name to *Señora Petty* before letting him garnish my paycheck off the back of his twisted rewrite of reality—but the fear was real. Because even empty threats have teeth when you're broke.

My financial situation was already precarious—more past-due bills than peace of mind—and the thought of paying for a lawyer, court fees, legal filings, and potential judgments started to press on me like a slow, crushing weight.

The gravity of it all hit me in waves. First came the disbelief. Then the rage. Then the creeping sense that this was exactly the kind of game he wanted to play: bleed me dry, wear me down, and twist the narrative so badly that the victim looked like the aggressor.

He wasn't just suing me.

He was trying to erase what he did by bankrupting the woman who dared to call him out for it.

In true Jason Lewis fashion, he didn't just come at me with a lawsuit—he also tried to twist the whole thing around and paint himself as the victim. His signature move: filing a retaliatory protective order. It was textbook Jason. Get accused of something? File a mirror claim and scream, *She's the real threat!* It was pathetic, but he was banking on someone in the justice system being too checked out to notice.

He had tried that with Sharon and failed. He tried it with Christen too, and failed. In fact, in all of the retaliatory protective orders Jason ever filed, none were ever granted by a judge. *That is literally the only positive thing I can say about the Oklahoma legal system in this whole story.*

At the Protective Order hearing, I showed up armed with my newly acquired Legal Aid attorney, Jesse Oakley Felmley, and a stack of truth. Jason showed up with his usual cocktail of smug and slimy. And let me tell you—watching him try to convince a judge that I was the one who needed to be restrained was almost impressive in its delusion.

But the judge saw through him. His retaliatory protective order was denied. Just shut down. No protection for the monster this time. It was a rare moment when the system actually worked for me like it's supposed to. And even though it didn't erase the river of shit I was still wading through, it felt good—like watching a cockroach get squashed under the judge's gavel.

🔥

I knew I needed help. Fast. This wasn't going to be some cute little legal skirmish with strongly worded letters and courtroom etiquette. This was about to be a battlefield. So I did the only thing I could think of—I launched a GoFundMe. I needed a real-deal attorney, not just to hold my hand, but to walk into court and throw punches on my behalf.

I'd been lucky enough to have Legal Aid during the protective order mess, but civil defamation? That's a whole different beast. Unpaid attorneys run screaming from that kind of thing, and honestly, I didn't blame them. Taking on Jason Lewis in a civil suit was like volunteering to juggle chainsaws while blindfolded. The stakes were high, the hours were long, and the payout was nonexistent.

But without a lawyer, I was stuck. Just me, Google, and the increasingly horrifying realization that *if I didn't find someone soon, I'd be walking into battle solo—armed with nothing but a handful of women who would testify he hurt them, blind rage, and my MacBook Pro.*

⁂

They say a person who represents themselves has a fool for a client—and baby, slap a jester hat on me and wheel me into court with a kazoo. I had no legal training, no courtroom experience, and zero clue how to file a motion—but I did have a burning sense of justice, a stubborn streak a mile wide, and a little something else I got from my mom: the ability to hold my damn head high, even when I was scared shitless.

By then, I'd learned the only real defense against a defamation lawsuit is the truth. And the truth? That's protected by the First Amendment of the United States Constitution—the very first one of those motherfuckers. That's why I thought I could represent myself. The flyer was true. Painfully, provably true. And if truth is a defense, then I was holding the sharpest damn weapon in the room.

Sure, I was wildly out of my depth. But I've got a decent vocabulary, a weird skill of public speaking, and just enough caffeinated delusion to pretend I belonged there. If confidence is 90% faking it, then consider me a professional impersonator. That courtroom got the discount aisle Elle Woods experience—no fancy law degree, just a mouthy Okie in Chuck Taylors and very real pit stains trying not to puke on the spot.

So there I stood—half-lit by blazing conviction, half-hoping I wouldn't cry or throw up—armed with my timeline and the truth. No passed bar exam, no power suit, no seasoned attorney whispering in my ear. Just me, representing a fool who knew too damn much to stay quiet.

Owning what I did and taking the hit for the flyer managed to calm most of the pissed-off survivors—but not Sharon. Sweet Jesus, not Sharon. And that one fucking hurt.

Sharon became an extension of Jason—another head of the same monster.

This was Sharon. Founding member of the Unicorn Club. Survivor of the same demon. She'd once told us how he made her prep her own body for an autopsy—literally. The same woman who sobbed through group therapy sessions with Christen and me. The same woman I believed had clawed her way out like the rest of us.

So imagine my face when I saw her comment on my Facebook post about the flyer: *"Leave that poor man alone."* I felt like the air got sucked out of my lungs. *"Poor man?"* This was the same man who terrorized her. Who made her scrub herself raw in bleach. And now she was siding with him?

At first, I tried to make sense of it. *Maybe she was just confused. Maybe it was some backwards trauma response.* But then came the knife twist.

I was at the Creek County Court Clerk's office, trying to track down records of Sharon's past abuse—trying to help prove my flyer was true (the only defense in a defamation case)—when the clerk looked up at me and said, *"You just missed her. She was just here. Her protective order is no longer valid. She dropped it."*

That moment felt like a knife straight to my kidneys.

Not only was she putting herself right back in harm's way, she was sabotaging my case against the man who hurt both of us. It was betrayal in broad daylight. I wasn't just being stabbed in the back—I was being stabbed in the back by someone who once sat beside me in battle.

And as if that wasn't enough, we later found out she had not only dropped her original protective order, but this was actually the second protective order she had filed against him in the last two years—and dropped. Twice she had gotten far enough to ask for protection, and twice she had chosen to let him right back in.

Then came the Florida vacation. While Christen and I were still trying to hold him accountable, Sharon was taking money out of their business account—twice as much as she was entitled to—and off vacationing in Florida like none of it was happening. When Christen asked her about the missing money, Sharon didn't explain or apologize. She threatened legal action. So Christen shut it down. She closed the account, dissolved the LLC, and kept the business she had built long before Sharon ever came around.

And when Sharon resurfaced after Florida, she came back with a brand new story. She claimed she had seen Jason again. *Ugh.* That he had almost killed her. *Double Ugh.* And then came the real kicker: she blamed me. She said that because of my *"loud mouth,"* she couldn't tell anyone about what he did. That because I had spoken out so publicly, nobody would have believed her. In her mind, I wasn't just part of the problem—I was responsible for her injuries.

Instead of taking accountability for her weak moment of returning to her abuser, she blamed me—her fellow survivor who had once stood beside her.

She admitted to something else too—something that hit and stunned me like I was Chris Rock at the Oscars. While the three of us were in Mexico on our Unicorn trip, sharing a tiny cruise ship stateroom, Sharon was laying there, three feet away, flanked by Christen and me in our little twin beds—her face lit up by the glow of her phone—texting the man who had hurt us all. Sending him selfies. Making sure he knew he still had her. While we were trying to heal, she was feeding him updates. Keeping him informed. Keeping his grip tight.

But finally, my little red dirt miracle happened. With the owner of the music studio willing to testify, and the incredible Jessie Felmley representing me for free, a judge granted me and my daughter a protective order against Jason—for a full year.

It felt like proof that light could find me. A rare moment where the system actually worked. For once, somebody in charge believed me, probably mostly because I had a credible witness who happened to have a swinging dick (*that matters in Oklahoma*). And I had nothing left to lose.

It wasn't a fairy tale ending. But for that moment? I had an unexpected glow-up from the universe. I had the law on my side. *Or so I thought.*

Chapter Eight

Corruption Castle

"Every Sunday's getting more bleak, a fresh poison each week." —
Hozier, "Take Me to Church"

Walking into the Pawnee County Courthouse for the first day of my defamation hearing felt like stepping into a lion's den—a huge "holy shit" moment where I half-expected the legal system to swallow me whole. By some miracle, it didn't devour me on the spot.

The building was yellow brick, chipped in places, like it had been through things it wasn't allowed to talk about. Inside, everything creaked. Floors, doors, even the benches—which looked suspiciously like old church pews, like someone raided a sanctuary clearance sale.

In my usual spot—the one where I used to sit while supporting the other girls—I noticed a single clipped fingernail on the floor. And I swear to God, it was always there. Visit after visit, same little crescent. I started to think of it as my quiet, harmless courtroom companion—just waiting for someone to finally come sweep it away.

There was an elevator that ran straight down to the old jail in the basement, which felt a little too on-the-nose for what I was walking into. The main courtroom had four tall windows that should've brought in beautiful light, but instead were draped in mangled mini-blinds that looked like they'd been salvaged from a cheap apartment during a windstorm. And in front of the judge's bench stood the American flag and the Oklahoma flag, one on each side like they were cosigning the whole charade.

The whole place felt stuck—like time had passed it by but nobody noticed. Or cared.

Jason was represented by his new best friend and shiny new business partner, Joshua Kidd. They had started a personal injury law company together, with Jason as its Chief Operating Officer. Imagine that. The man who injured so many was now profiting from other people's pain, brokering settlements like some twisted karmic joke. I knew damn well he wasn't paying a dime for Josh's services—either it was free or one of those greasy barter deals between bros. Meanwhile, my "attorney" was a real catch—if you needed marketing help, a Halloween pumpkin carved, or a cheesy '90s piano love song played on command. As for courtroom strategy? I was flying blind with nothing but a paralegal friend and the kind of grit that grows when you're too pissed to give up.

And yet... I liked Josh. I know how that sounds. But just like I had compassion for the women in Jason's life, I had a weird soft spot for anyone tangled in his web—even his lawyer. Josh didn't see the monster yet. He was being played. I saw him the way I once saw myself: smart, kind, decent—and neck-deep in someone else's bullshit. And somewhere in the chaos of all that trauma, I thought maybe if I could just show him who I really was, he might see through the act.

We exchanged a lot of emails during that lawsuit—some tense, some surprisingly human—and I always tried to thread a little truth into mine. I wasn't just defending myself. I was trying to hold onto the best parts of me.

Here's one I sent him on May 3, 2016:

> *Hey Josh, I just wanted to say that in any other universe, I think you and I would be buddies. There aren't many people on this earth that I don't like, and I hate that I'm not allowed to like you!! You're a really good attorney and I really hope you find nothing but success in life. Mean that.(Except in court against me, of course.)I just wanted to give you a heads up—since you were kind enough to do the same—that I filed an amendment to my answer today*

in Pawnee. I also added a counterclaim of Civil Assault, Civil Battery, and Intentional Infliction of Emotional Distress. I sent it to your PO Box this afternoon.

Take care,

Karrah Youngblood

He didn't respond to that one, but I like to think it landed somewhere past his lawyer armor. Josh was loyal to Jason—at least on the surface—but every now and then I'd catch a crack. A subtle nod. A moment of decency. I found out he was a left-handed, music-loving liberal with cats. Basically, my people. Jason's fake alpha-male schtick doesn't stick long with someone like that, no matter how thick the bro-code runs.

I remember one day standing outside the door of the courthouse waiting to go in, I looked at him and said, "I think you're gonna like me one day, Josh." He grinned.

In another world, we could've been friends. But in this one, we were just two people trying to survive the same manipulative bastard from opposite ends of a courtroom.

Now, I'm not saying every woman who's dragged into court by her abuser dreams of a courtroom hero, but I think we all hope for at least one adult in the room. Turns out there wasn't. Just a quiet understanding that the system wasn't designed to protect someone like me.

Enter the final boss: Judge Patrick Pickerell.

Just saying his name makes my eye twitch a little.

From the second I walked into his courtroom, something felt... off. Like the whole thing was tilted. I couldn't put my finger on it at first, but it was a vibe. The kind of vibe where you realize you've accidentally walked into a courtroom cosplay event where everyone's pretending it's fair, but the script's already written. It felt like showing up to a knife fight with a pool noodle—*while the judge handed Jason a fucking machete.*

And this wasn't just a gut feeling—it was public fucking record. *The Tulsa World* had already exposed Judge Pickerell in a story that should've disqualified him from judging a middle school debate team, let alone a civil trial. Turns out he'd been indicted for asking—drumroll please—Jason's own attorney, Joshua Kidd, to lie for him in an unrelated case. So yeah. My abuser's lawyer was the judge's alleged former co-conspirator. And I was supposed to believe this was fair?

So there I was. A woman with no formal legal training, a haunted past, and a strong sense of right and wrong—up against a predator, his lawyer, and a judge who might as well played strip poker with them both.

This definitely wasn't like what happens on *Law & Order.*

So no, it wasn't just fear of losing the case that kept me up at night—it was the slow realization that I may have never had a fair shot at all.

The odds? Shit.

But the stakes? Everything.

Welcome to Oklahoma, motherfuckers.

Chapter Nine

Silenced.

"No one dared disturb the sound of silence." — Simon & Garfunkel, "The Sound of Silence"

The defamation lawsuit came with a shiny new bonus feature: a temporary restraining order against me and my flyer. Or, more accurately, a full-on gag order designed to wrap my mouth in red tape and shut me the hell up. I wasn't allowed to show anyone the flyer. Couldn't talk about what was in it. Couldn't even say Jason's name out loud. *Yeah. You read that right.* I was legally barred from processing my own trauma. The court literally told me I could not speak the truth of what happened to me—not to my friends, not to the public, not even to a therapist trained to help people like me.

They also made me take down my GoFundMe page—the one lifeline I had to maybe, possibly hire an actual attorney. Without it, I was left on my own, broke and emotionally shattered, trying to fight a lawsuit with nothing but a list of formerly battered witnesses, a sharp tongue, and nothing to lose.

My income hovered just above the food stamp cutoff, which meant I wasn't poor enough for help and not remotely rich enough for the type of lawyer that I needed. Meanwhile, Jason strutted in with his business partner and bestie, Joshua Kidd, suiting up on his behalf.

I was just a pissed-off woman with Wi-Fi and a spine.

They wanted me to stay quiet.

And the more that motherfucker tried to silence me, the louder I got.

The injunction hearing should have been simple—just a hearing to determine if I could keep the flyer up or not. But instead, it spiraled into a full-blown trial about whether the contents of the flyer were true. Here's the kicker: that's not how injunction hearings are supposed to work. But in "Corruption Castle," the rules were more like vague suggestions.

Representing yourself in court is a terrible idea. Representing yourself against the man who beat and raped you? That's its own circle of hell. Especially when you're not a lawyer, you're still visibly traumatized, and your only strategy is to stack enough evidence to impress the judge into seeing the truth—or at least guilt them into caring.

I was fumbling my way through the legal process, clutching my growing binder like it held the Constitution, a miracle, and maybe a Xanax. I was an absolute nervous wreck, but I showed up anyway, and I opened my mouth even when it shook.

There I was, cross-examining my abuser.

Not watching from the sidelines. Not being spoken for. I was the one holding the evidence, asking the questions, looking him dead in the eye. No one had trained me for this moment, but somehow I'd arrived in it anyway—heart pounding, voice shaking, determined not to flinch.

And it felt empowering as hell.

He had to sit still and behave himself. He had to answer my questions. And I got to ask him the ones I'd been dying to ask for years. He couldn't interrupt. He couldn't gaslight or threaten. He couldn't throw things or back me into a corner. He had a judge watching him and a 9-inch-thick slab of antique Pawnee County oak between us, courtesy of the courthouse's creaky-ass witness stand. I was protected by architecture and the Constitution, baby.

This time, he couldn't touch me. And I could finally hit back—with the truth.

I could taunt him. I could press him. I could get him where it hurt. I got him to admit he hadn't filed taxes in years. I got him to admit he wasn't actually able to fly a plane. I had so many questions I didn't even think to ask in the moment—because I wasn't prepared for any of it—but I still walked away with a string of confessions and contradictions that he couldn't wiggle out of. *I wondered what Josh Kidd thought of his business partner being in tax trouble?* Something tells me that wasn't disclosed when they formed the L.L.C.

One moment I'll never forget: I handed Jason an email he himself had submitted as evidence, and told him, "Please read the whole thing." It was the one where I sarcastically asked for $10,000 to pay for rectal surgery. (Yes, rectal surgery. No, not a metaphor. Yes, this is my actual life.) He told the court he thought I made it up. That I was lying. Like having your body torn apart is just a cute little exaggeration.

He smirked. I didn't.

I didn't have a law degree. But I had a mountain of emails, screenshots, and firsthand accounts of his pattern of cruelty. The judge kept interrupting—"One question at a time, Ms. Youngblood." "Don't interrupt the witness." "Let him finish." But when the witness is the man who made you afraid to sleep with the lights off, it's hard to keep it courtroom polite. I wasn't there for pageantry.

At one point, I asked, "Did you say she's not a cunt like you, so no beating is required?"

He just said flatly, "I didn't write that."

Cool. Just your name on the email and your exact cadence and hateful-ass tone.

It was like cross-examining a ghost—one that lied and shapeshifted every answer. He denied everything. Even the things that had already been proven. Assault? Never happened. Threats? Misunderstood. Protective orders? All just bitter women with a vendetta.

When I brought up the message he sent my boss claiming I was a danger to children and a drug addict, he flat-out denied it. When I mentioned a woman he beat in Arkansas, he said she didn't exist. When I asked him if a detective was actively investigating my rape case, he shrugged and said no one had ever contacted him. Just pure, unchecked delusion.

He proceeded to tell the court my flyer had ruined his life. That it damaged his precious reputation. But I pulled out a screenshot of a recent Facebook post where he was bidding on a private plane. "Outbid by two dollars," he bragged in his caption. *Picture of financial ruin, my ass. Imagine that, bidding on a plane you can't even fly.*

Still, I knew I had to show the judge that the flyer was true, and not, in fact, defamation. But here's the twist: I wasn't supposed to have to prove that that day. We weren't supposed to be calling witnesses at all—it wasn't that kind of hearing. And Christen, who was sitting quietly in the courtroom just to support me, definitely hadn't signed up to take the stand. But the way things spiraled, I didn't have a choice.

So I called her.

She wasn't prepped. I wasn't ready with questions. But she showed up, like she always had. That day, she was the only other woman willing to sit beside me in court. And when the moment came, she told the truth.

I asked her, "If you saw the flyer today, would you have dated Jason Lewis?"

She answered honestly: "No, I would not."

That one honest sentence—so simple, so pure—turned out to be the nail in my coffin. The judge took it as proof that the flyer had damaged Jason's reputation. Because women might read it and decide not to date him. *God forbid.*

I didn't win that day. But I didn't lose everything either. I got to look him in the eye and say what needed to be said. And even if I didn't walk out of there with a courtroom victory, I walked out knowing I hadn't backed down.

If the courtroom hadn't already felt like a rigged game, the ruling that day sealed the deal. Not only was I barred from showing the flyer or talking about the facts on it, the judge issued an injunction that muzzled me completely. Past, present, and future. I wasn't allowed to say his name out loud, or repeat any of the facts on the flyer. I wasn't allowed to tell my story. I wasn't even allowed to say his name to a therapist. Let that sink in: I was legally forbidden from speaking aloud about my own life—because it involved him. Because he didn't like that.

The judge's official ruling was a masterclass in First Amendment gymnastics. He acknowledged that free speech was important... and then said it came with "responsibilities and consequences," comparing it to the Second Amendment, like my words were weapons that needed regulation. *(Fun fact: they were. But only because the truth hits hard when you've spent your life avoiding it.)*

He said the purpose of my flyer wasn't "before him that day." Which is wild, considering the entire point of the flyer was the reason I was standing there being gagged in the first place. He said the issue at hand was whether Jason was entitled to an injunction. And because someone "vaguely familiar" with him might have a worse opinion of him after reading it? Boom. That was enough for the court to decide he was the one being harmed.

He claimed my actions hadn't followed "the proper method" for protecting the public. *As if there's some official Pamphlet on "How to Warn Women About a Predator While Following Proper Etiquette."* What should I have done? Posted Yelp reviews? Filed a customer service complaint? This was years before every major city had its own "Are we dating the same guy?" Facebook group, designed to warn women of shitty men.

He was concerned that the women on the flyer might not have wanted to be identified. And you know what? That was fair. They hadn't signed up for that. That decision had been mine—desperate, defiant, and maybe flawed—but it came from a place of protection, not malice.

Still, none of those women had chosen to be his victim either.

The idea that their anonymity mattered more than their safety? That their silence was preferable to my voice? *That stung.* Because while I might've taken a risk by including their photos—albeit with black bars over their eyes as my attempt to protect their identities—Jason was the reason those stories existed in the first place. And yet, somehow, I was the one being punished—for speaking up, for speaking out, for trying to prevent anyone else from becoming the next name on a list.

Instead, the judge said Jason had "barely" met the requirements to get an injunction—but that was good enough. He ruled that the potential harm to me—a broke single mom with PTSD and no legal counsel—was less than the potential harm to Jason—a grown man who had repeatedly harmed women and still somehow got to play victim.

In the end, it didn't matter that I had proof. It didn't matter that I had lived it. All that mattered was that I made noise. And in a courtroom like that, noise—especially when it comes from a woman like me—is the ultimate threat.

I walked out of that courthouse legally forbidden from telling my story.

But I'll tell you this now: that story didn't die that day. It went underground. *It smoldered.*

And eventually, it would come roaring back.

By that point, Sharon had vanished from group therapy. She was back in Jason's clutches, and it broke my heart more than I could admit out loud. Christen and I kept going, though—kept showing up to Cynthia's cozy little office with our battle scars and our blunt honesty, doing the work. Cynthia had been our soft place to land for a while. A neutral ground. A place where we didn't have to explain why we were still unraveling.

But then Wildfire happened. And Cynthia didn't approve.

She didn't say it outright at first. She said things like "You two are feeding off each other's trauma" and "Maybe your friendship isn't helping either of you heal." But we could feel it—the subtle shift, the judgment creeping into the room like a cold draft. She saw our friendship not as fuel for survival, but as some kind of trauma loop. *Like our bond was a symptom instead of a strategy.*

We begged to differ.What she called co-dependence, we called sisterhood. What she saw as re-traumatizing, we saw as reclaiming our power—together. Cynthia wanted us to go our separate ways, to process alone, to quietly untangle the grief without each other's noise. But Christen and I had been through hell side-by-side. We weren't about to turn on each other now just because it made our therapist more comfortable.

So we did what any two strong, stubborn, traumatized best friends would do.

We fired her. Kindly. Respectfully. But firmly.

We closed that chapter and walked out of her office for the last time, knowing we'd rather navigate the chaos together—flawed and furious and unfiltered—than pretend our healing needed to be palatable for anyone else.

Besides, I wasn't allowed to say his name in therapy anymore, so what was the point really?

The day the Department of Human Services (DHS) came knocking, I was standing in my living room with my daughter, surrounded by half-packed suitcases and neon snorkels. We were literally in the middle of packing for a cruise to the Bahamas when the DHS social worker showed up at my door to investigate me for child neglect. I still remember the baffled look on her face when she took in the chaos of vacation prep behind me.

Because dragging me into court, slapping a gag order on my truth, and twisting the legal system into a fucking knot wasn't enough... Jason decided to go for the jugular: my kid.

Except, of course, he didn't have the guts to do it directly. That wasn't his style. He sent one of the many women he manipulated—Stephanie Winters—to file the bogus DHS report on his behalf. Jason didn't even have to lift a finger. He let his enablers do the dirty work for him. It was his pattern. If one head of the monster didn't get the job done, he just grew another.

Or as Christen put it so perfectly: "He didn't just abuse you—he built himself a whole fucking army of flying monkeys to abuse you." Ugly. Delusional. Selfish. And honestly, how the hell did he get so many women to line up and defend him? Christen said it best: "I think for some women, deep down, they just hate each other."

And Jason knew exactly how to tap into that.

Every. Single. Time.

The timing of the social worker visit almost felt like a joke. Rayne and I were packing for our mother-daughter cruise to Atlantis, the Bahamas resort with water slides, dolphins, and drinks served in coconuts. I had saved up for months. It was supposed to be just the two of us, unplugging from the chaos and living our best damn lives. The second the DHS worker stepped inside, I apologized for the mountain of beach towels, travel-sized sunscreen, and scattered flip-flops taking over the living room couch. If she had any heart at all—and she did—she probably knew within five seconds that this kid wasn't neglected. She was about to head to paradise.

Still, the poor lady had a job to do. She was kind and professional, the kind of person who's probably seen things in homes she can never unsee. She interviewed us separately. I hovered by my bedroom door, practically holding my breath, straining to hear how Rayne would respond. Not because I was scared—okay, maybe a little—but because it mattered.

"What's the worst punishment your mom gives you?" the social worker asked.Without hesitation, Rayne answered, "Sometimes she takes away my YouTube."

That was it. No beatings. No screaming matches. No horror stories. Just the trauma of temporarily losing access to Minecraft tutorials. The nerve of me.

Needless to say, DHS didn't take my kid that day. In fact, the final report read:

> "OKDHS recommends individual counseling for the natural mother would benefit her as she goes through the stressful situation with her previous boyfriend/stalker."

So while Jason was busy trying to weaponize the system to break me, all he really did was hand the state of Oklahoma one more reason to see me for what I actually was: a protective, overextended, exhausted single mom doing her best.

And in case you were wondering, my little neglected daughter had the time of her life on that cruise.

But Stephanie wasn't the only woman Jason had out there doing his bidding. There was also Trisha Skinner. Yet another woman Jason had manipulated into believing I was some jealous, psycho ex who was obsessed with him. I knew his game, so I reached out to her directly—hoping, maybe, I could save her from becoming the next one.

I messaged her:

> Hi Trisha, I am one of the countless victims of Jason. Did he hurt you?

Her response:

> "Just 2 let u know I would NEVER be a a friend with a psycho BITCH like u.... I have heard all about u and read all ur text messages 2 Jason. The games u girls play with this poor man is sickening and makes me ashamed that people like u girls act this way... it's VERY sad. U ALL really need 2 GROW up and learn how 2 act 2 people. And my relationship with this person is none of ur FUCKING business. PLEASE LEAVE ME OUT OF

> UR GIRLS MESS I DON'T HAVE TIME FOR IT OR ANY OF U!!!!!"

Bless her heart, thinking I wanted him back and was just some jealous ex. Gosh, he was good at spinning his bullshit.

I replied:

> Good luck to you then. I'll pray for you.

She shot back:

> "Don't need your prayers, he's a WONDERFUL man. Maybe you need them."

I said:

> "Maybe you need to visit the Oklahoma State Court Network's website."

She replied:

> "I already have, sweetheart."

I responded:

> "I am not your sweetheart. I was sincerely looking out for another girl. I am blocking you now because he is probably gonna kill me or my kid now that I've checked on you."

She fired off:

> "You guys are all just psycho crazy bitches to me."

I told her:

> "One of these days you will see that we aren't. Sorry he has you fooled. Later gator."

Her response:

> "I don't think so."

I ended:

> "He has three girlfriends in Iowa and you think he is wonderful. Amazing. Good luck to you. I mean it. Please don't get me killed, I am begging you."

And her parting shot:

"I don't think he would waste his time on you."

Jason Lewis and his loyal soldiers tried daily to shut me up. Gag orders, injunctions, threats to my livelihood, bogus DHS reports—they threw the whole damn kitchen sink at me. But here's the thing about silencing a woman like me: it never really works. My voice didn't disappear. It got sharper. Smarter. Louder. And no matter how many times the multiple-headed monster tried to bury me in paperwork and bullshit, I kept showing up. I kept speaking. Because the truth doesn't go away just because it's inconvenient. And neither the fuck will I.

Chapter Ten

Karrah Youngblood, Graphic Designer At Law

"I got smarter, I got harder in the nick of time." —Taylor Swift, "Look What You Made Me Do"

Amid the legal circus (thirteen hearing dates between April and August—yes, I counted), something wild was happening: I wasn't shrinking. I was growing. The more Jason tried to knock me down, the more determined I became to raise my voice—and my damn standards.

Thirteen soul-sucking trips to the courthouse meant thirteen days off work, thirteen mornings spent packing evidence and Advil, and thirteen afternoons muttering "fuck this" under my breath while navigating the 108-mile round trip to Pawnee. Sometimes I had a co-pilot—Christen, my sister Amie, her fiancé David (aka Earth's Kindest Human), my childhood friend Jaclyn, my high school friend

Kevin Sparks, or Don Hardcastle, my biker neighbor who sounded like he should be in a Western and pretty much acted like it. And some days, it was just me. One woman, one car, one mission: survive the flaming dumpster and somehow still pay the bills.

Ironically, all that sink-or-swim energy started fueling something unexpected—my career. I was still working part-time at 20/20 Sign Design, a family-owned shop a few miles from my house, turning architect sketches into clean, high-resolution, full-color apartment maps. It was oddly soothing. But I'd start each morning by checking court dockets like I was scanning for landmines. Miss one hearing? I'd lose by default. And you can bet your ass Jason was banking on it.

Too bad for him—I'm annoyingly punctual and deadline-driven.

My mouthiness on social media didn't go unnoticed. I was practically allergic to silence, and Jason's attorney made it his personal mission to threaten me with Contempt of Court about every other week. "If she posts again, we'll file sanctions." "If she violates the gag order, we'll seek ten grand in penalties." They were relentless. But so was I.

Every new threat just made me dig in harder. The more they tried to muzzle me, the more determined I became to speak. I wasn't just surviving—I was sharpening.

Then came a plot twist in my professional life: after three months, the little design firm I was cushily working part-time for got bought out. The new company inherited two sign installers, two fabricators, a boatload of signage contracts, one busted van, and two designers—Jay (a formally trained design wizard) and me (a self-taught rebel with something to prove). We got plucked like claw machine prizes and moved to a sleek new shop in Midtown Tulsa.

My old boss introduced me to the new one with, "This is Karrah—she's good for spellchecking." *Coolcoolcool. Love a first impression that screams "barely useful."*

Ashley, the in-house designer, had the dream office next door—massive printers, a vinyl cutter, a film printer, all the "adult crayons" you could dream of. Rumor had it they weren't planning on keeping me past six months—it was actually in the contract when they made the acquisition. So, I launched Operation: Make Karrah Indispensable. Sure, Ashley was talented and sweet, but I had a kid to feed—and a lot of pent-up fire from years of being bullied by a monster to channel.

I didn't get many assignments at first, but the ones I did? I worked like my future depended on them—because it did. We were only allotted an hour of design time per job, and I wasn't good enough or fast enough to keep up. *Yet.* So I took projects home every single night. After working a full day and teaching piano students in the evenings, I studied YouTube tutorials, devoured Adobe books, and walked in each morning acting like I'd whipped it together over a cup of Folgers. I was hustling hard enough to sweat caffeine.

Two months later, Ashley got transferred. I got her office, her printers, and her throne. Suddenly, I wasn't the third wheel. I was helping run the damn department.

By the time they put my name on the door, I didn't need to sneak my work home or fake my confidence. I could crank out clean, client-ready work in an hour flat—and still make it look easy. Somehow, while juggling court threats and trauma flashbacks, I had become a full-time, completely self-taught corporate designer.

And just to rub a little glitter on it: in October, Comic-Con hired me to carve a pumpkin for William Shatner. I skipped meeting him so my daughter, could meet Evanna Lynch, the actress who played Luna Lovegood in the Harry Potter franchise. *Mom Points.* Zero regrets.

Jason could keep throwing lawsuits at me. Meanwhile, I was stacking wins. My daughter was happy. I was thriving. And all those contempt threats? Still hanging in the air—uncollected, unenforceable, and completely unable to stop me.

Despite having Jason blocked on every platform known to man, I knew his creepy little network of flying monkeys was still out there, refreshing my Facebook like it was a stock ticker. Lurking. Watching. Hoping to catch me breaking. *Bless their hearts. I didn't break. I doubled down.*

If they were going to stalk me anyway, I figured I might as well give 'em a show. Social media became my pressure valve—equal parts therapy and battlefield. I posted with purpose. Sometimes rage, sometimes wit, always fire. Posts like "I hope the cops haul his ass off before he hurts anyone else" and "I'm trying to save his next victims" were probably not technically court-approved... but they were true, and *dammit, that counted for something in my soul.*

Of course, Jason and his lawyer lost their minds every time I posted something. They threatened injunctions. They filed sanctions. They sent stern letters with phrases like "willful violation" and "contempt of court." I was racking up Contempt threats like they were Starbucks stars. But no matter how many legal scare tactics they hurled my way, they never once scared me into complete silence. Because here's the thing: when someone has already tried to destroy your life, there's not a whole lot more they can take.

Eventually, I realized something oddly empowering. I could call Jason an abuser every damn day of the week. Yeah, the court might fine me ten grand for each "offense" for violating my gag order, but there was no way in hell I'd ever fork over a single cent to that man. *I'd eat glass first. Figuratively. (I've never been suicidal. I'm way too stubborn to die quietly.)*

I kept talking. Kept posting. Kept resisting the urge to shut up and sit down like a "good victim." I lived for being an absolute thorn in Jason Lewis's ass. Getting under his skin became a full-time hobby.

Bullying the bully became my therapy. I decided I'd run my mouth until someone physically shut it—and I'd open it again with stitches if I had to.

The threats became background noise. Like a buzzing fridge you learn to tune out. My truth was louder. And even if no one else ever saw those posts... *he did.* And that, frankly, was enough.

Because I may have been gagged by a court order. *But he really underestimated my mouth.*

What he never accounted for... was me.

Karrah. Fucking. Youngblood.

The same girl I've always been — and no bully was ever going to change that.

Chapter Eleven

Heather

"Hello? Is there anybody in there? Just nod if you can hear me." —Pink Floyd, "Comfortably Numb"

When Jason married Heather in Iowa—wife number four—it didn't come as a shock. What did surprise me was how fast she enlisted in his campaign against me. She didn't hesitate. She didn't ask questions. She just picked up her keyboard and stepped right into formation—another soldier in his online firing squad. Another head of the monster.

Heather started showing up to court dates to testify on his behalf, promising to testify that I was causing Jason "financial duress" by refusing to stay quiet about the abuse. From her seat across the courtroom, she'd glare at me with something colder than contempt—like she wanted to erase me. And as much as I tried to ignore it, those eyes got under my skin. There was no mistaking it: she had chosen the wrong side, *as if choosing mine was an option. It wasn't. Not then anyway.*

But Heather didn't stop at court. She was straight-up bullying me on Jason's behalf on social media. Soon, her entire family joined in—loud, aggressive, and terrifying. Her brother publicly discussed how—and where—they might dispose of my body. Not in private. Not in anger. Casually. On social media. Like it was a sport. Like I was nothing more than an inconvenience they were brainstorming how to get rid of. They were literally posting Facebook comments about using her brother's backhoe to dig my grave.

I reported it to the police, of course. I had a protective order in place. I did what I was supposed to do. I went to the Sapulpa Police, hoping for protection—maybe even justice. But they brushed it off. Told me it wasn't a "real threat." As if plotting a woman's murder online didn't qualify as alarming unless they actually showed up with a shovel.

So once again, I was left exposed. Unprotected. Vulnerable. The system that was supposed to keep me and my daughter safe offered nothing but indifference. And indifference, when you're being hunted, feels like betrayal.

The hardest part? I could see so much of myself in Heather. So much of Christen. Even Sharon. She was a pretty registered nurse, a single mom from a close-knit Minnesota family—someone I probably would've liked under different circumstances. Being in the medical field, I assumed she was kind, empathetic, and strong. And that's exactly what made her a perfect target for Jason.

Jason always picked women like us—women with soft hearts and big capacities for belief. Women who made excuses for bad behavior and held onto the hope that love could fix someone. Heather walked straight into the same hell we had to fight tooth and nail to escape. And knowing that made it all harder to watch.

So I stopped taking her hatred personally. Not because it didn't hurt—it did—but because I knew where it came from. I knew what kind of stories she'd been told about me. I knew how charming Jason could be when he wanted to rewrite history.

But more than anything, I knew what was coming. I knew, deep down in that sick place where dread lives, that it was only a matter of time before he hurt her. And when he did, I wanted her to remember that I never fought her. I didn't retaliate. I didn't stoop. I just waited.

I hoped—*foolishly, maybe*—that one day, Heather would see me clearly. Not as the enemy. But as someone who knew the road she was on. As someone who might just be waiting at the end of it with an open door. *I knew Jason would hurt her if he hasn't already, it's just a matter of how bad.*

It was only a matter of time. It was inevitable. *It's the only thing that makes him happy.*

Chapter Twelve

Defeated

"When the fire's at my feet again, and the vultures all start circling, they're whispering, 'You're out of time.' But still, I rise." —Katy Perry, "Rise"

By that point, I was so emotionally and physically depleted, I'd started tossing certified letters from Jason's attorney straight into the pile of unopened bullshit. I couldn't stomach one more envelope full of legal threats from a man who used the court system like a weapon. Still, despite the exhaustion pressing down on me like wet cement, I kept checking the Oklahoma State Court Network like it was my part-time job. If they were going to try and steamroll me, I wasn't about to let it happen without a fight.

Then came November 2, 2016. I was deep in design mode at my Tulsa office—building a billboard for some client who had no idea their design chick was currently in a legal hellscape—when my phone rang. It was Lisa Rainwater, my paralegal friend-turned-lifeline.

"Why didn't you come to court today?"

Cue confusion, panic, and a sudden wave of nausea. *What court?* I had an actual letter from Joshua Kidd's office—where 2nd had been crossed out and replaced with 9th. The Oklahoma State Court Network said November 9th, too. Hell, I'd even called the court clerk on November 1st just to triple-check. There was no court on the 2nd. It was so clear—until it wasn't.

They'd tricked me.

Just like they did to Christen a few months earlier, they lied to get me to miss the hearing. With no one there to defend me, the judge issued a default judgment. I lost.

I lost the defamation case. I was officially gagged forever.

Not because the evidence was on their side. Not because I'd done anything wrong. But because I'd been ambushed—again—by a system that seemed more interested in punishing my courage than in seeking the truth.

To make the sting worse, Jason's attorney used that very same day to file for monetary damages. And, as if that wasn't enough, they demanded I take out a full-page ad in the newspaper apologizing for my "actions." *You know—my crime of warning other women that a violent man was, in fact, violent.*

I was gutted. Betrayed. Furious. They had to cheat to beat me, and it worked.

But even as that ruling sucker-punched the breath out of me, I wasn't fully down. There was still something burning in me—rage, yes, but also a deep refusal to disappear quietly. As the sun set on Jason's so-called victory, he strutted online like a rooster, thumping his chest to anyone who'd listen. My phone blew up with screenshots of his bragging. People who barely knew me sent me messages with his smug Facebook posts. He was gloating, full of himself, declaring he'd "won."

And I? I couldn't say a damn word. The gag order permanently kicked in. I owed him money. I owed him silence. *I owed him nothing, and yet—here I was, muzzled and gutted while he crowed about the kill on Facebook.*

By early December 2016, I was operating on fumes and whatever was left of my pride. I had filed a motion to vacate the default ruling—my Hail Mary to undo the November ambush. I knew I'd been set up. Lied to. I just needed the court to acknowledge it and give me a fair shot. But when I showed up for the hearing, rain pattering against the windows and dread pooling in my stomach, I got a big fat nope.

Judge Pickerell denied the motion to vacate. The default judgment would stand.

I'd lost.

Again.

But instead of slapping me with the full set of consequences then and there, Judge Patrick Pickerell did something I wasn't expecting—he hit pause. Maybe he saw how outmatched I was. Maybe he actually felt something resembling pity. Whatever the reason, he decided not to rule on damages that day. Instead, he gave me one last thread to cling to: "Come back in January," he said, "with an attorney."

So let's recap: I was being forced to spend money—money I didn't have—to pay a lawyer, just to find out how much more money I was going to have to pay my abuser.

The math wasn't mathin'. None of it was mathin'.

But somehow, on that freezing gray morning, in the middle of a system designed to chew women like me up and spit us out, I left the courthouse with the tiniest ember of something I hadn't felt in weeks: forward motion. My brother-in-law David drove, and I stared out the window in silence while *Rise* by Katy Perry played on repeat. Someone had sent it to me the night before. Said it reminded them of me.

I didn't feel like a warrior. I felt like roadkill with mascara. But I took it in anyway. I let the words crawl into my chest. I let the rain blur the outside world just enough to keep my tears private.

Because despite everything, I wasn't done.

As empowered as I wanted to feel leaving court that day, the truth was: I had no attorney, no money, and no damn clue how I was going to survive the next legal round. I'd just been told to go hire someone—someone expensive—so they could help calculate how much I now owed the man who abused me. *That's not justice. That's a hostage negotiation with better lighting.*

And even I had to admit, I couldn't handle this on my own. Not anymore.

That's when the universe—via one of my adult piano students—tossed me a weapon disguised as a name. My student was secretly learning piano to surprise his wife for their anniversary, and when he heard what I was up against, he referred me to an old friend from his University of Tulsa debate team. His name was Taylor Burke, a real-deal attorney. A courtroom killer with a conscience.

He was perfect. He was also way out of my financial league.

I started scrambling. My 401(k) wouldn't release my funds unless I quit my job, which wasn't an option. So my sister Amie and I hit the road like Girl Scouts on a mission, visiting every aunt and uncle in a single day, hustling like we were selling Blue & Gold Sausage to keep my dignity alive. We raised a few thousand dollars that way—but it wasn't enough.

That's when another friend stepped in and launched a GoFundMe on my behalf. I was mortified. Humiliated. The idea that I needed charity to defend myself against a predator made me want to crawl into a hole and disappear. But then something wild happened.

People showed up.

Students. Friends. Strangers. My entire community formed what felt like a human wall around me. Small donations rolled in with messages like "We believe you" and "You're not alone." For the first time in a long time, I didn't feel like I was drowning. *I felt seen.*

But before the court could crush me with another blow by ruling that fundraising for an attorney violated the gag order—another miracle landed in my inbox.

RJ, a friend from high school I hadn't spoken to in years, reached out privately. He told me he had a daughter. And he couldn't stand the idea of a world where women were punished for trying to protect each other. So he quietly covered the rest of the retainer. No fanfare. Just support.

That moment—the realization that I would actually be able to stand in that courtroom with a real lawyer beside me—hit harder than any judgment. It wasn't just about the money. It was about dignity. It was about not being forced to fight this monster alone anymore.

Naturally, Jason and Joshua Kidd tried multiple times to hold me in contempt of court for raising money to defend myself. Because how dare I try to level the playing field? *How dare I refuse to let them steamroll me one more time?*

It's like they weren't realizing that every punch they threw only built the army behind me. They thought humiliation would break me—but it became the thing that pulled my people in closer.

And this wasn't just my fight anymore.

This was a fight for women everywhere—for every woman who's ever been silenced, sidelined, or dragged through the mud for daring to tell the truth. If I didn't back down, maybe others wouldn't either. Maybe the ripple would catch, and someone else would find their voice because I used mine.

By December, the harassment wasn't slowing down—it was escalating. The online threats just kept coming, getting more twisted, more personal, more terrifying. They weren't just coming for me anymore—they were targeting my daughter. Body-shaming her. Calling me fat. Comparing me to John Wayne Gacy because I "looked like a clown" in my photos—apparently smiling while surviving makes you a psychopath in their eyes.

But the most chilling part? The talk of the backhoe. It kept coming up.

Jason's new wife's family—her father and brother—had these casual, public conversations about how and where to bury me. Like it was a group project. They discussed logistics. Equipment. Disposal. And they weren't trying to hide it. *And deep down, I truly didn't hold it against them because I knew the most manipulative bastard alive was pulling the strings.*

It wasn't just harassment. It wasn't just bullying. *It felt like a goddamn countdown.*

I became paranoid. And I had every right to be.

I was doing everything the court told me to do. I had a protective order. I had followed most of the rules and jumped through all the hoops. And still, I was being hunted. Online. In my hometown. In my inbox. I started scanning every unfamiliar truck that drove by my house. I jumped at shadows. *And I felt like if I didn't scream loud enough soon, someone might actually dig a hole and try to put me in it.*

So I made another police report. I wrote it in my own rushed handwriting on 12/10/16. It wasn't professional. It wasn't polished. But it was desperate. Honest. Raw.

> "My protective order is a joke. I dated Jason Lewis for three weeks in 2014. He is a monster and has DOZENS OF VICTIMS. Will he have to kill me before you arrest him? He has tried to get me fired from 2 jobs, tried to file false reports with DHS, and I'm tired of being bullied. And recently he and his wife are using social media to stalk and harass me and my 9-year-old daughter. Jason

> Lewis II is currently suing me for defamation because I had the audacity to report his crimes and warn other women about his cruel behavior. Six protective orders can't be wrong."

That's what I wrote. That's what I handed them. And still, no one did a damn thing.

The police saw the threats. They saw the screenshots. They saw what was happening.

And they shrugged.

Again.

The system that claimed to protect women like me was too busy twisting its wrists, looking for ways not to get involved. I was begging to be believed, begging to be heard, begging someone to stop this man before things escalated further.

But nothing happened.

So I braced myself for what I already knew: *if help was coming, it wasn't coming from the people with badges.*

⁂

Taylor Burke's law office didn't just whisper "prestige"—it dripped it from the ceiling. I've been in a lot of professional spaces. I've worked in corporate environments, been around C-suites, and grew up with a mother who mingled with every class of society imaginable. But this place? It was sexy. Even for a law office.

Everything was deliberate—the lighting, the marble tile, the silence that felt expensive. The boardroom had a massive, glossy mahogany table that looked like it had hosted depositions, power plays, and billion-dollar negotiations. The leather-bound chairs were the kind you sink into and immediately wonder if your posture's good enough to sit in them. It didn't feel stuffy. It felt powerful.

I remember the way it felt when the receptionist offered me and my sister a cup of coffee.

Not in a paper cup. Not as an afterthought.

Real mugs. Warm hands. Polite tone.

And it made me tear up. After everything I'd been through—being silenced, threatened, called a liar, turned into a villain—I didn't realize how starved I was for a basic gesture of care.

That coffee tasted like safety. Like someone saying, *you deserve to be treated like a human being.*

Then came Taylor.

He looked every bit the part: tailored suit, sharp eyes, commanding presence without being arrogant. The kind of man who could dismantle someone's bullshit with a sentence and never raise his voice. No billboard lawyer. No ambulance chaser. No gimmicks. He was the real deal.

I laid it all out—what Jason had done, what the court had done, what I was still living through. Taylor listened without interrupting, taking notes, asking precise questions. I watched the subtle shift in his face—the tightening jaw, the furrowed brow—as he realized just how thoroughly I'd been screwed over.

And then he said he'd take the case.

On January 17, 2017, Taylor officially filed his entry of appearance in *Jason Lewis vs. Karrah Youngblood.* I wasn't just some girl showing up alone anymore. I had representation. I had backup. I had someone who knew how to fight fire with fire professionally.

That night, I sat down and drew him a goofy cartoon of himself, with a Superman logo peeking out from under his dress shirt. It wasn't about flattery. It was gratitude, pure and simple. He was my newest hero.

He told me to stay quiet for now, to let him work. And I did. I hated it, but I did. The gag order still had me legally muzzled, but outside that courtroom, the volume was rising anyway.

Friends. Survivors. Strangers. Even people connected to Jason's life were speaking out. Andy—the stepdad of Jason's daughters—started sending me updates from Iowa. From his International Harvester in the middle of a cornfield, he was texting me things like, "He's unraveling," and "You're really getting under his skin." *I'm telling you—truth has a funny way of finding allies in the most unexpected places.*

The silence wasn't silence anymore. It was a pause before the storm. And behind that storm was a growing crowd of people who made me feel like I finally wasn't fighting this alone.

If Jason thought he could isolate me, *he truly forgot who I am.*

🔥

Meanwhile, right around the time Taylor Burke started rocking Jason's world, in January 2017, it happened.

The thing I knew was coming. The thing I'd braced myself for. The thing I prayed wouldn't happen, even though I knew it would.

Jason beat Heather.

He was arrested for domestic abuse with strangulation. He impeded her airway. There was sexual assault. The charges were sickening, but not surprising. Not to me. He'd done it again. *Someone should have tried to stop this from happening. Oh wait.*

Heather—the same woman who once sat across the courtroom from me, glaring daggers, testifying on Jason's behalf, claiming I was causing him "financial duress"—was now in the exact same hell he'd dragged the rest of us through. And it was even worse than I imagined.

He tortured her. He burned his initials, *JCL,* into her skin with a cattle brand. He beat her with dowel rods. He used battery clamps. Toothpicks under her fingernails. Forced her to take wine enemas, milk enemas. Held her down and forced himself down her throat until she vomited—and then made her clean it up.

It makes me want to vomit just typing it.

And somehow, amid that horror, I still knew what came next: she was going to reach out.

I don't remember what I was doing when Christen texted me, but I remember exactly how it felt. She said Heather had made contact. Not with me—yet—but with her. Heather was still tangled up in his lies, still trauma-bonded, still convinced I was the enemy. But something in her had started to shift. The reality of what Jason had done to her was punching holes through his version of the truth.

I immediately unblocked her on Facebook. The same woman who once threatened to help bury my body had become the next in a long, horrific line of survivors. I knew that message would come. And when it finally did—"Message request from Heather"—I didn't hesitate. I opened it.

We bonded immediately. I didn't have to forgive her, because I never really held anything against her in the first place, knowing just how good Jason is at manipulating people. *Welcome to the Unicorn Club, Heather.*

By March, I was in motion again—head down, bills paid, doing the damn thing. I was working as a corporate designer with real weight behind my design portfolio: Boeing, Lockheed Martin, the U.S. Army Corps of Engineers, even the Tulsa Police Department. After school, I was still teaching piano to kids with sticky fingers and wild imaginations. I was caring for my disabled dad, raising a third grader alone, and surviving a smear campaign with more stamina than most war zones.

And Jason? Jason was still obsessed with destroying me.

He'd already reached out to every job I had, firing off emails accusing me of being a danger to children and a drug addict. He was relentless—convinced that if he just shouted the lies loud enough, someone would finally believe him. Then he took things offline and old-school.

A few months earlier, after one of those soul-draining court appearances, I needed a drink. Only I'm not much of a drinker, so I stopped on my way home to get a little nugget of weed. It was Oklahoma, pre-legalization. On my way home, I got pulled over. I was arrested for possession of a controlled substance and spent 45 humiliating minutes in Creek County Jail.

Forty-five minutes. *Let me be clear: I had now served more jail time in Creek County than the man who raped me.*

That should have been the headline.

Instead, a few weeks later, Jason took that moment and weaponized it the way only a petty, cruel man with a god complex can. He printed yard signs. Twenty-four by eighteen-inch corrugated plastic yard signs with my mugshot on them, topped with the phrase: "KNOW YOUR NEIGHBOR." I was smiling very big in my mugshot (because I always told myself to take advantage of the opportunity if it came) and was wearing street clothes, so the picture did not really look like a booking photo.

He placed the signs all over town—like lost dog posters, only I was the villain he wanted everyone to fear. He even put one in the parking lot of Rayne's elementary school, even though her protective order states Jason is not allowed within 1,000 feet from her.

I found out about the signs while sitting in my sleek office in Tulsa, sipping coffee and chipping away at a stack of work orders. My phone rang. It was my cousin Bradley. "There's a sign with your face on it by my office," he said. "I took it down."

I stared at the phone, stunned. *What the hell was he talking about?*

Then more messages came in. Strangers started messaging me on Facebook.

"I saw a sign with you on it. I took it down because it looked like something done to bully."

"Are you okay?"

"This is wrong."

He didn't stop with the signs. Jason had also created a companion Facebook page and website: knowyourneighbor.info. The page was public, and people started commenting right away—"Sounds like this poor girl has a stalker."

"This isn't exposing someone—it's harassment."

"That guy's crazy. This looks like revenge."

Even strangers could smell it. They didn't see a warning sign—they saw a red flag. And the whole town noticed.

But what he didn't count on—what he never seems to factor into his plans—is that a LOT of people know me. Rayne's teachers and principal had known me for years. They saw me every day. They knew the situation. They knew who I was, what I was up against, and who the real threat was. They didn't just roll their eyes at the sign—they publicly defended me.

And so did strangers. Strangers took the signs down with their own hands.

Because the truth is, no one in their right mind was going to believe I had a drug problem. At the time, I was a professional designer, a piano teacher, a single mom, a caregiver, and a woman under siege. *I didn't have time for a drug problem. I didn't have the luxury of unraveling. I was too busy holding the damn line.*

Jason thought he could humiliate me into silence. But all he did was prove exactly who he was. Again. And this time, it gave me the ammunition I needed to file for a new protective order violation—for me and for Rayne since he was within 1,000 feet from her classroom.

He could cover the town in signs, but in trying to make me look bad, he only made himself look worse.

Unfortunately, the signs were not found in violation of my protective order. According to the Sapulpa Police, Jason is allowed by my daughter's school.

⸙

Even in those dark days—when I felt like I was screaming into my pillow—little glimmers of light kept finding their way to me. Sometimes it came from strangers. Sometimes from unexpected corners of my life. And sometimes from the exact people you'd never expect to show up when most of your own family doesn't.

One by one, people started to take interest in the amount of bullying I was withstanding. Not everyone knew the full story, but they could feel the weight I was carrying. And they did something rare—they cared.

Like the kind woman at the UPS Store who printed my court filings without question. Sometimes, she wouldn't even charge me. She'd just slide the envelope across the counter, give me a look, and say, "Give 'em hell, kid." And I sure tried. I had to.

Parents of my students defended me, even when they were given every reason not to. They saw the smear campaign, the gossip, the way people turned their backs—and they stood beside me anyway.

And the teachers at my daughter's school? They quietly kept watch. Made sure she was okay. Protected her in ways the police wouldn't. They didn't make a show of it. They just did it. Because they knew.

Those quiet acts of belief—those everyday rebellions—held me together more than anyone will ever know. They were the proof that even when systems fail and silence closes in, human decency still exists. And sometimes, it shows up when you least expect it... but exactly when you need it.

In the spring of 2017, something finally happened.

Jason was arrested—not for what he did to me, and not even directly for what he did to Heather—but for violating his probation in Christen's case by beating Heather on the very last day of that probation. All he had to do was stay out of trouble. Just keep his hands off another woman long enough to finish his deferred sentence. But Jason couldn't help himself. He never could. The violation was black and white. And this time, Corruption Castle had no choice but to react.

Later that year, in April, Heather came to testify at Jason's probation violation hearing. She brought her daughter. The night before court, she met me and Christen for the first time in person over dinner—and had an actual, honest-to-God good time. We laughed, talked, and shared stories. Trauma forged something unexpected between us: not just understanding, but trust. It was nice to watch Heather realize with every minute passing that she genuinely liked the girls Jason strategically programmed her to hate. She was very humble and grateful to be around us. Over dinner, I learned Jason was planning a lavish vacation with the money he was going to win from his lawsuit against me. *Like hell he was.*

The next morning, we showed up together. And we didn't come quietly.

We walked into that courthouse with Christen, Lisa Rainwater, Tess Maune (a local TV Reporter), and a full camera crew waiting in the hallway. When Jason stepped off the elevator and saw us—me, Heather, Christen, a reporter with a microphone, a tiny little hormonal army—the look on his face made it almost worth all of this. No time to posture. No smirk. No false charm. Just pure deer-in-the-headlights. *I smirked.*

It wasn't justice—not yet—but it was a moment.

And I took it.

Inside the courtroom, Heather took the stand and didn't hold back. She testified under oath that Jason had choked her, sexually assaulted her, threatened her life, and left her traumatized. Right there in front of Judge Pickerell. She talked about her PTSD, the night terrors, the loaded weapon she kept by her bed, and the fear she lived with every time she closed her eyes. It was everything the rest of us had said for years—now entered into the court record. Josh Kidd, scrambling, tried to discredit her by bringing up a hot check she wrote as a teenager. *Pathetic.*

Out in the hallway after court, Heather stood in front of Tess Maune's camera and said something that echoed in my bones:

"Don't stay. They won't change. They'll never change. You'll end up dead. You've got to get help and get fixed. You've got to get through it."

I wasn't allowed to be interviewed because of my gag order. But I stood right there, off-camera, watching her tell the world exactly what I had spent years being silenced for. It was surreal to watch her—this woman who once hated me—now speaking truth to cameras, confirming everything I had screamed into the void for years.

Christen told the cameras, "Ninety days in jail after nineteen hearings associated with my attack and he finally gets held accountable. It is so sad he continues to hurt other women and it has come to this."

I loved that Christen and Heather were both able to get a little justice in one swoop. One woman's pain validating another's survival. A monster finally cornered by the very women he thought he'd broken.

Or so I thought.

Because even with the testimony, the cameras, and the arrest warrant, nothing was promised. If the judge ruled Jason had violated his probation, he could face a whopping ninety days in jail. Ninety days—for beating, branding, and torturing another human being.

But even so—it was movement. A crack in the foundation. A ripple in a system that had done nothing but fail us.

No, it didn't make things right. But it made him sweat. And for once, *he* was the one being hunted.

So there it was. After everything—after the protective orders, the legally forced silence, the threats, the stalking, the beatings, the branding, the torturing, the rapes—Jason was sentenced to 90 days in jail for violating his probation.

Ninety days. *That's what it cost him to brutalize yet another woman while still on thin ice for the last one.* It wasn't justice. But it was something. For a moment, it felt like maybe—*maybe*—he would finally be forced to sit still and feel the consequences he'd dodged for so long.

But even that was too much for the system to hold onto.

He served just a few days.

He was able to get the judgment overturned and was released on appeal—just walked right back out like the whole thing had been a clerical error. He didn't serve ninety days. *He barely served a weekend.* And just like that, the pressure evaporated. The crack in the wall sealed itself back up. The gavel may have dropped, but it didn't echo for long.

I wish I could say I was surprised. But this was Oklahoma. This was Pawnee County. *This was motherfucking Corruption Castle at its finest.* This was exactly how it had always worked.

They gave him one more slap on the wrist and sent him back into the world to hurt again.

But here's the thing: *this time, he didn't walk out unnoticed.* This time, the world had started paying attention. This time, we at least had a news story.

And not just any story—we had a 6 and 10 o'clock news story. A reporter on our side. An article to share stating Jason was an abuser, that I didn't even have to write.

But even then, it wasn't who it should've been.

Over the years, I'd reached out to Lori Fullbright more times than I can count. She's a well-known reporter in Tulsa, constantly branding herself as a "victim's advocate"—a trusted voice for domestic violence survivors. But for all her advocacy, I couldn't get her to care about my case for five minutes. Always a "let me know how it goes" reply. Never a call back. Not one ounce of curiosity about the system dragging me through the mud and protecting the man who hurt me and so many others.

In total, I reached out to Lori Fullbright 9 times. It was one of the most helpless feelings—knowing that someone who publicly claims to fight for victims didn't think *this* situation was worth her time. And it made me wonder: who exactly qualifies for a victim's advocate? Do we have to be dead first?

Instead, Channel 6 sent Tess Maune. Tess—the reporter best known for covering catfish noodling tournaments and outdoor stories. Ironic, but fitting. Jason was an animal, after all.

And to be fair, Tess showed up. She looked us in the eye. She pointed a camera at the truth. While the so-called advocate couldn't be bothered to listen, the outdoor reporter was the one who put our pain on record. I don't mean to sound ungrateful for Tess, she was a godsend. I don't even mean to sound bitter about Lori Fullbright. It wouldn't be fair to remember her for the one person she didn't help vs. the many she did. I just felt like if the "victim's advocate" didn't care, nobody ever would.

So no, this wasn't justice. It wasn't even close. *But it was pressure.*

It was documentation.

It was something the system couldn't erase, and Jason couldn't manipulate.

He may have walked out of jail like nothing happened. But the story stays forever.

KOTV News On 6 Featured the article:

> A Pawnee County man who pleaded guilty to assault and battery and was sentenced in 2015 could be headed back to jail in the same case after being accused of

new crimes in Iowa. Jason Lewis calmly walked into a Pawnee County courtroom Friday. Court records show that in 2015, he punched a woman in the face twice, then grabbed her by the hair and shoved her face into a gravel driveway. Lewis pleaded guilty in that case and was given an 18-month deferred sentence. In court Friday, Lewis's attorney argued that his probation had ended in March, but the state claimed Lewis violated the terms of his sentence when he was arrested in Iowa. Lewis is now facing charges of domestic abuse assault that impeded the flow of air or blood, as well as harassment. He is accused of choking and beating his current wife in December 2016. The harassment complaint stems from a phone call in January 2017, where his wife says Lewis threatened her life. "I'm a survivor, yeah," his wife said. She testified at Friday's hearing but asked not to be identified. "I have PTSD, night terrors, sleep with a loaded weapon... worry for my kids constantly," she said. She told the court Lewis had threatened to kill her numerous times and had violently abused her both physically and sexually. The woman said it took her months, but she finally left—and urged other women in similar situations to do the same: "Don't stay. They won't change. They'll never change. You'll end up dead," she said. "You've got to get help and get fixed. You gotta get through it."Court records show Lewis has had four protective orders filed against him by three different women. He has also filed protective orders against some of those same women. On the stand, Lewis denied every allegation. His attorney said he would prefer not to speak to the media until the court issues a ruling. If the judge determines Lewis violated his probation, he could be sentenced to 90 days in jail. A decision is expected May 5.

Chapter Thirteen

I'm Speaking.

"And I didn't even have to use my AK — I gotta say it was a good day."
—Ice Cube, "It Was a Good Day"

I don't mean to fill his inbox for the next 20 years, but if you need a good lawyer, come to Downtown Tulsa, Oklahoma and get Taylor Burke on retainer. Because when Taylor stepped into that courtroom the first time, the entire energy shifted. He didn't puff up or get loud—he didn't have to. He just calmly, surgically reminded the court that what had been done to me was in direct violation of my First Amendment Rights, and that they'd better be ready to defend it.

After over a year of being legally muzzled, after drowning in contempt filings, legal gymnastics, and courtroom gamesmanship, I finally got my day—the one where Taylor Burke stood up and fought back in full force.

He argued that the gag order—officially titled a *Total Restraining Order*, which sounds more like a sci-fi death sentence than a civil ruling—wasn't just harsh, it was unlawful. He made it plain: under the law, this kind of equitable remedy never should have been entered. It wasn't just inappropriate. It was unconstitutional. It was unlawful. It was in clear violation of my First Amendment Rights. The whole judgment had to be undone, according to the laws of the land, and we had to start over.

And then, on June 30, 2017, the state's grip around my throat finally loosened.

After *441 days* of living under a state-issued muzzle, Judge Patrick Pickerell granted a partial summary judgment in my favor. It was typed in black and white, stamped, sealed, and signed—but to me, *it felt like someone had finally handed me oxygen.*

"The Temporary Restraining Order entered by this Court on April 15, 2016 and extended on May 19, 2016, is vacated, dismissed, and considered null and void. IT IS SO ORDERED, ADJUDGED, AND DECREED."

I read it twice. *Then again.* I'd spent over a year being legally forbidden from telling the truth about the man who beat and threatened me. A year where *speaking out could land me back in court—or in jail.*

And now? *That crushing legal weight lifted off my chest.*

For the first time in over a year, I could legally say what needed to be said: Jason Lewis is a serial abuser. Jason Lewis is also a fucking monster.

And I said it. *Out loud.*

Sure, I still had to tread carefully. *I knew how quickly the legal system could turn on me.* But for the first time in a long time, I wasn't gagged. *I didn't feel small.* And nobody—**nobody**—could punish me anymore for warning another woman.

I had my voice back.

And damn it, I was going to use it.

As if the universe had been holding its breath right alongside me, waiting for the gag order to be lifted, something unexpected happened that very same month—something that felt like fate finally throwing me a bone. A young neurosurgeon named Dr. Baird walked into my office looking for a logo design for his new Telehealth startup.

We hit it off immediately—professionally and personally. He was smart, driven, visionary. I was smart, driven, battle-hardened. *We got each other.* Dr. Baird would sit behind my desk and watch me design his graphics in awe. *This man that literally makes humans walk again was impressed by little ole me.* And after a few successful projects, he asked me to join his team full-time.

Just like that, piano lessons and creative side hustles gave way to a shiny new title: Vice President of Creative Operations.

I was plucked up out of my cool office like I had just been drafted to the Medical NBA. Suddenly, I was surrounded by brilliant colleagues, building branding systems, designing functional apps, and dipping my toes into the nerdy, mystical world of database architecture. It was corporate design at a whole new level—and I was thriving in it.

Dr. Baird appreciated my work—and more importantly, he paid like he meant it. That salary bump wasn't just financial relief; it was the validation I never knew I needed. Rayne and I celebrated the only way we knew how: by *doing things that made us feel alive.* I sprung for front-row seats to the Tulsa Oilers—our local pro hockey team—sitting close enough to see the scars on the Head Coach's face. We hit museums, visited family across state lines, and—because *fuck it*—we took not one but two vacations to the Bahamas. We'd earned it.

For the first time in my adult life, money wasn't a constant pressure. I still took on freelance projects here and there such as making sports highlight films for local high schools—just enough to keep my creative muscles stretched—but I no longer had to hustle to survive. *I could finally breathe.*

And when the pandemic hit, locking down the world and flipping everything upside down, I was already a remote work pro. While others scrambled to adjust, I was already in my groove, headphones on, tabs open, making stuff on things and solving problems in leggings and messy buns.

Turns out, when life tries its hardest to break you, you don't just bounce back. Sometimes you come back louder. Smarter. Stronger. *Somehow I kept upgrading. Jason didn't realize he was making me a better, stronger person during this whole ordeal.*

I even slowly found my way back to the gym. *It was time to finally take care of my body the way it deserved.*

By then, something had already begun stirring in me long before I even had the words to name it. I remember watching Colin Kaepernick take a knee during the national anthem and feeling an immediate, gut-level understanding. Plenty of people around me were pissed off, but I wasn't. *For the first time, I realized the flag didn't represent me either*—not the me, who stood in police stations and courtrooms, begging for help while my abuser walked free. I was living in a country promising "truth, justice, and liberty for all," yet painfully learning just how conditional those promises really were.

Look, I wasn't Black. I wasn't a man facing the brutal, daily reality of racial injustice. But I sure as hell knew what it felt like to stand in front of people with badges, speak my truth, and watch them look straight through me—as if my pain didn't matter, as if my life didn't matter. And if this was how dismissively they treated someone like me—a white woman with a big supportive family and community connections—*how much worse was it for Black men and women, for people of color who never even got that thin, fragile layer of protection?*

Colin was using his First Amendment rights, something I now cherished more deeply than ever. After years of being legally gagged, sued, and threatened for daring to speak my truth, I knew exactly how precious—and fragile—that freedom was. I understood why he knelt. *Because the system doesn't protect everyone equally.* For a lot of us, the flag doesn't represent safety; it represents a broken fucking promise.

And by October 2017, the world erupted into a collective *fuck this* moment. The #MeToo movement wasn't some quiet exchange between women anymore—it was a goddamn roar. Harvey Weinstein was being dismantled, piece by disgusting piece, and powerful men everywhere were finally being dragged into the harsh sunlight. Brave voices poured across red carpets and newsfeeds. Oprah was giving spine-chilling speeches. Celebrities wore black in solidarity. It was a reckoning—raw, overdue, and loud.

And there I was, in Oklahoma, freshly ungagged, watching it unfold with a weird mix of pride and paralysis. *The world was finally saying, "We hear you. We believe you. Speak your truth."* But after being silenced for so long, my own voice felt like a stranger. Years of gag orders and threats had conditioned me to overthink every word, bracing for punishment. Even though I'd blatantly violated my gag order multiple times, the fear had become muscle memory. *Now that I could finally speak, I had to relearn how to actually be heard.*

I believed every single woman who came forward—every tweet, every story, every gut-wrenching detail—because I knew. *I knew. I fucking knew the gut-twisting courage it took.* Admitting you were assaulted, harassed, manipulated—saying out loud that a man hurt you—is one of the hardest damn things a woman ever faces. The minute those words leave your mouth, the burden becomes yours to carry, prove, and survive. There's nothing empowering about the first time you say it; *it's fucking terrifying.* And the world doesn't always reward your truth with justice.

While the world finally opened its ears to survivors, I was still pulling my voice up from underwater. That twist of irony—watching the world rise just as I learned to stand again—hit me hard. The *Time's Up* slogans marched right past me like a parade I wasn't sure I'd been invited to, even though I'd been one of the first to decorate my float. But buried inside that weird, tangled feeling was something restless: my voice, finally stretching its legs—*rusty as hell, but ready.* And this time, *no court order would shut me up.*

As my voice got stronger, I couldn't stop seeing everything differently. Women carry culture, incubate life, hold entire communities together—every woman, in every culture. White women especially have proximity to both privilege and marginalization, and the power to either reinforce injustice or push for equality. But entitlement can blind us, isolate us, trick us into thinking we're better, and chip away at our innate compassion. If the system could silence me—a white woman with every kind of support—*what unimaginable damage was it doing to people without even my minimal protections?*

I thought back to how officers looked at me when I reported violations of my protective order, dismissing my words, treating my pain like it was negotiable. *How much fucking worse was it for young Black men, Black women, all people of color—hell, anyone who wasn't a straight white male?* For people whose truths never even reached an ear willing to listen?

That's when I deeply understood why movements like #Black-LivesMatter exist. I had felt just a sliver of systemic injustice, yet even that small glimpse was enough to open my eyes wide. I'm not equating my experience—but once you've stood within a broken system and seen how effortlessly dangerous men evade consequences, *you can't help but notice exactly who the system was built to protect—and who it doesn't.*

Let's be real: *if Jason Lewis had been a Black man in Oklahoma, committing the same brutalities, he wouldn't be walking free.* He wouldn't get endless appeals, loopholes, and second chances. He'd be locked away for life in the Big Mac—the McAlester State Penitentiary in McAlester, Oklahoma, that is.

That realization didn't just give me empathy—it gave me a perspective I'll carry forever. Because once you see how uneven justice is served, *you can't unsee it.* You listen closer. You speak louder. And you stand stubbornly beside those the system fails—*long before it ever fails someone like me.*

The late Congressman John Lewis referred to the act of taking peaceful, nonviolent action to challenge injustice and create positive change as *Good Trouble.*

At some point along the way—without even realizing it—I found myself right in the middle of it.

Proudly.

I was determined to keep raising my volume.

And if that made me trouble?

Good.

By the end of it, I had probably been told a thousand times—by people I loved and trusted—to just move on. Let it go. Focus on my future. Wait until he hurts the *right* woman.

No.

I was the right woman.

And I am the wrong woman—the one who didn't stay quiet. The one who couldn't.

If there's anything I hope you take from this, it's that we have to stop encouraging women to move on just to keep the peace. Sometimes standing up for yourself *is* the peace. Sometimes speaking the truth out loud is the only way forward.

For me, it's been the best therapy.

Making little-girl Karrah proud by finally sticking up for her—that shit goes deep.

Chapter Fourteen

Registered

"I'm the bad guy... duh." —Billie Eilish, "Bad Guy"

Meanwhile, up in Iowa, Jason's trial for beating Heather bounced around the court calendar like a cursed pinball—scheduled and rescheduled five damn times between May 2017 and May 2018. He was originally charged with Domestic Assault by Impeding Air Flow, which basically means he choked her until she nearly died. At one point, they even tacked on a felony sexual abuse charge, which he of course denied. And in the end, like always, he avoided prison again. But this time, something stuck.

Jason ended up pleading guilty to First Degree Harassment, which sounded like a slap on the wrist—until you realized what it meant under Iowa law. Because unlike Oklahoma, Iowa actually kinda gives a shit about women. Their harassment statutes are some of the strictest in the country, and since Jason's charge was determined to have been "sexually motivated," he was officially required to register as a sex offender.

Let me repeat that: The man who raped me was now a registered sex offender. Not for what he did to me, of course. But for what he did to Heather.

And that designation, even if it came years too late and for a crime that didn't include the word *rape*, felt like another little sprinkle of justice. Heather's pain became the lever that finally yanked back the curtain. His name would now sit next to other infamous predators in the national database. Jason Lewis, right there in the same category as Larry Nassar, Harvey Weinstein, Jeffrey Epstein. No, he wasn't rich or powerful, but he shared the same rotten DNA—the entitlement, the manipulation, the violence, the trail of devastated women.

This wasn't just about Heather anymore to me. It was a moment for every woman he ever terrorized, silenced, manipulated, or discarded. For Christen. For Sharon, even if she hates me. For the mystery Arkansas survivor. For every girl who said yes when she meant no because he made her feel like she didn't have a choice. For every one of us who got told we were crazy, dramatic, vindictive, unstable. *We weren't. We were fucking right.*

He'd always managed to slither out of consequences, and in a way, he still had—he wasn't behind bars. But this time, he couldn't escape the label. "Sex Offender." Not for the next 10 years anyway. It followed him like a scarlet letter stitched across his chest, a permanent record of the monster he swore he wasn't.

For once, the legal system said it out loud.

On August 17th, 2018, The Times Citizen reported:

A Hubbard man who was charged last year with choking his wife, pleaded guilty this month to first-degree harassment and is now required to register as a sex offender.

Jason Carl Lewis II, 43, was arrested April 6, 2017, on a charge of domestic abuse assault – impeding the flow of air or blood, which is an aggravated misdemeanor. According to court documents, in December 2016 he grabbed his wife by the throat and choked her until she nearly blacked out. In May last year, Lewis's charges were amended to add one count of third-degree sexual abuse, which is a class C felony. Then–Assistant Hardin County Attorney Denise Patters filed the additional charge. Court documents state that on the same day Lewis was accused of choking his wife, he also performed a sex act against the victim's will or by force.

Lewis pleaded not guilty to the charges. His trial was scheduled and rescheduled five times between May 2017 and May 2018.

On Aug. 5, Lewis entered a guilty plea in Hardin County District Court. In the agreement, filed on Aug. 6, he pleaded guilty to first-degree harassment, an aggravated misdemeanor. In court documents, Lewis admitted that between Oct. 9 and Dec. 22, 2017, "with the specific intent to intimidate, annoy or alarm my wife, and with a sexual motivation, I did communicate to her a threat to kill my wife." The following sentence was outlined:

- *A two-year sentence at the Iowa Medical and Classification Center in Oakdale, Iowa, which was suspended*
- *One year of probation*
- *A $625 fine, plus a statutory surcharge and court costs, as well as any restitution*
- *Lewis must submit a DNA sample to the Iowa Division of Criminal Investigation*
- *A no-contact order currently in place between Lewis and the*

victim will remain in effect for five years and includes anyone she lives with and any members of her immediate family, and the order can be extended.

- *Lewis must register as a sex offender for 10 years*

Shortly after his arrest last year, Lewis appeared in court in Pawnee County, Okla. Prosecutors there alleged that Lewis's Iowa arrest constituted a violation of the terms of a 2015 guilty plea from a case in which he was accused of assaulting a woman. A Pawnee television station—News on 6—reported that at the time, Lewis had four protective orders against him by three different women. In court he denied all allegations against him.

After the conviction hit the news, KOTV Channel 6 posted the story online. I was scrolling through the comment section—half-dreading, half-hoping to see something human—when my breath caught in my throat. A woman named Carisa had commented under the article.

"This man beat the shit out of me in Arkansas in the 90s."

I stared at the screen in stunned silence. *There she was.*

Carisa.

The woman Christen and I had been trying to find for years. The one he swore under oath right there in front of God and everybody didn't even exist. One of the elusive original unicorns of this entire story. I'd whispered her name in courtroom strategy meetings and scribbled her into timelines and dreamt of one day finding her, alive. *Because honestly, I wasn't sure she was. Not after what he did to me. Not after what I knew he was capable of.* For a long time, she felt more like a ghost than a real person.

But there she was—leaving a public breadcrumb for the world to see. No frills, no hashtags, just one brutal sentence that confirmed everything I had feared and everything he had denied.

It wasn't just me. It wasn't just Christen. It wasn't just Heather. He had been doing this shit since before dial-up internet. And now one of his earliest victims had stepped out of the shadows and joined the chorus. Whether she knew it or not, she was giving me something I didn't even realize I still needed: validation.

That single comment on Channel 6's webpage hit hard.

She was real. She had survived. And she was speaking.

Chapter Fifteen

Marci

"All you'll ever be is a faded memory of a bully." — Shinedown, "Bully"

When my friends started sending me screenshots of Jason's newest wife, Marci, I felt that old, familiar nausea churning up my throat. I didn't know her, but I knew her. I knew the type of woman he hunted—bright-eyed, single mom, trusting. Another pretty face about to get twisted into a headline. *I didn't want to be right.* But I knew I was. *We all did.*

I braced myself for the day she'd join our fucked-up little Unicorn Club. We had the champagne chilling, metaphorically speaking, because with Jason it's never *if.* It's *when.*

And *when* came in February of 2021.

News broke that Jason had been arrested in Iowa. And this time, the details were on another level. What he did to Marci made everything I'd endured feel like warm-up drills. This wasn't a rerun of his usual violence—it was full-blown escalation. The monster had sharpened his fangs.

To celebrate six months of marriage, Jason and Marci went "back roading"—the rural romance version of hell. The same way Jason celebrated my 36th birthday. He even grabbed a bottle of Banana Schnapps—his signature "panty remover" poison—the exact liquor he drank the night he punched me on the highway. *Some things never change.*

They ended up at a dive bar, where Marci kicked his ass at pool. And that was all it took. His fragile ego couldn't handle it.

While Marci was in the bathroom, Jason left and drove home. A kind bartender gave her a ride and dropped her off across the street from their house, where they usually parked on the grass. As she approached her car, planning to sleep there to avoid what she already knew was coming, she saw him. Sitting in his truck, waiting, staring at her.

He rolled down his window and asked, "What are you doing?"

"Nothing," she answered, trying to diffuse the situation before it exploded.

Without hesitation, he opened his truck door and punched her directly in the face, knocking her out cold.

She doesn't remember much after that. The next thing she recalls is being inside the house, waking up on the bedroom floor while Jason screamed at her—not because she was injured, but because she was bleeding on the carpet. *That's all that mattered to him: the fucking carpet.*

She crawled into the office and passed out again. When she came to, he was slapping her awake and calmly informing her that she was gurgling on her blood. Somewhere in that fog, he likely kicked her in the ribs. The pain was immediate and sharp when she came to. The injuries lined up with what kicking could've caused—but the details were blurred, buried under the trauma and the concussion that left much of that night a disjointed haze.

Somehow, she managed to get up and walk to the bathroom—and that's when she saw herself in the mirror for the first time.

Her face was completely unrecognizable. Swollen. Covered in blood. Four open lacerations that had to later be glued shut. Massive bruising around her throat. Her bright, beautiful eyes were lost under layers of swelling.

Her phone was on the bedroom floor where she had first passed out—but thankfully, her Apple Watch was still on her wrist. And that watch saved her life. She used it to call 911 and whispered one word: "Help." That was all she could manage.

She tried to escape out the back door and made it as far as the front sidewalk before he tackled her again in the deep Iowa snow. She's certain that brutal fall is likely what caused the compression fractures in her spine.

She truly believed she was going to die. But through the snow and the chaos, she saw flashing headlights barreling toward them. The officers arrived just in time.

He would have killed her that night. She has zero doubt.

Jason was arrested and charged with kidnapping, willful injury causing serious harm, assault causing severe injury, two counts of possession of a firearm by an abuse offender, domestic abuse assault with intent to inflict serious injury, and harassment. A goddamn rap sheet.

Her injuries were catastrophic. Four buckle-fractured ribs. One rib broken clean through on the other side. Two compression fractures in her spine. A broken nose. Four facial lacerations. A concussion. Possibly a traumatic brain injury she still grapples with today. And bruising so severe she was nearly unrecognizable.

When I saw the ambulance photo of Marci for the first time, I couldn't even locate her eyes. She looked like she had been through a war zone. Like she'd been attacked by ten men.

Even Christen couldn't take it. When she saw the photo, she shut down for days and wouldn't answer my calls. It wasn't just triggering—it was haunting.

Because this wasn't just another woman falling into Jason's web. This was escalation. This was the end game if monsters like him are allowed to keep getting away with it.

Could I have stopped this? Should I have fought louder? Shared more? Screamed sooner? I don't know. But the guilt sat in my chest like a brick.

That night, I showed my dad the photo and said, *"This is what the monster I've been fighting all these years is capable of. This is why I never shut up."*

And for the first time, I think people finally started to understand.

❧

It took less than two weeks for formal charges to hit. Jason had brutalized Marci so savagely that even the State of Iowa—a place that let him wriggle free before—couldn't pretend it didn't happen.

The *Eldora Herald-Ledger* ran the headline:

"Lewis Posts Bail."

Of course he did.

Jason was officially charged with:

- Kidnapping
- Willful injury causing serious harm
- Assault causing serious injury
- Two counts of possession of a firearm by an abuser
- Domestic abuse assault with intent to inflict serious injury

- Harassment

It was the kind of rap sheet that should've ended in flashing cuffs and a courtroom meltdown montage. But this was Jason. And somehow, there was always someone willing to throw money his way.

According to the article, a third party (that turned out to be his son) posted the $100,000 in cash (from their business account) for his bond. One hundred thousand dollars just sitting around for a man with half a dozen protective orders and a history of beatings, stalking, harassment, and worse. A man who already had a shiny new sex offender designation under his belt. *That kind of support was baffling to me.*

He was released on February 25, 2021, with an ankle monitor and pretrial supervision. As a registered sex offender, he had to register his address again. He was also slapped with a no-contact order—one that covered Marci, her home, and her immediate family. *A paper shield, basically.*

They made sure to note it in the article like it was some kind of victory: **"Lewis is subject to a no-contact order with his victim in this case,"** said County Attorney Darrell Meyer. *No shit.*

I read that line over and over like it was supposed to mean something. Like a monster follows rules. He'd been issued no-contact orders before. He'd violated them too. This wasn't new. It was déjà vu with much worse injuries and a bigger bail amount.

But at least this time, a judge *had* to see through it. There was no spinning that ambulance picture. This time, the charges were long, specific, and stacked—and they came with evidence that no human should ever have to look at, much less endure. *And still... he walked free awaiting trial.*

The *Eldora Herald-Ledger* wrote:

> **Lewis Posts Bail** *ELDORA – According to Hardin County Attorney Darrell Meyer, Jason Carl Lewis II made bail on Feb. 25 and is out of custody. He was jailed on alleged assault and kidnapping charges against his wife, Marci, on Feb. 15. Lewis, or a third party, put up cash in the amount of $100,000 for his bond, Meyer stated. Lewis is required to wear an electronic monitoring device and be on pretrial supervision to the Department of Correctional Services. As a registered sex offender, Lewis must also register his address with the Hardin County Sheriff. He is also subject to a no contact order with his victim in this case, Meyer said.*

Lewis was charged with:

- 1st Degree Kidnapping

- Willful Injury – Causing Serious Injury
- Assault Causing Serious Injury
- Dominion of Firearm/Off Weapon by Domestic Abuse Offender
- Domestic Abuse Assault with Intent to Inflict Serious Injury – 1st Offense
- Harassment – 1st Degree

Chapter Sixteen

The Hate Crime

"Honey, I've changed so much since I last saw ya." —Chinchilla, "Little Girl Gone"

A few days after Jason was charged with brutally assaulting Marci, something unprecedented happened: Hardin County Attorney Darrell Meyer added an eighth charge—Assault with Intent to Inflict Serious Injury with a Violation of Individual Rights. Our abuser was being charged with a hate crime against women. The first case of its kind to be heard in a U.S. courtroom.

He was finally being charged for being the serial abuser I had said he was for years.

But let's be clear who helped push that door open. It was Christen.

Christen called the Iowa District Attorney herself. She asked the blunt question that most prosecutors would never touch: Why is it never attempted murder? Why is it never charged as a hate crime?

If Jason had been out there exclusively raping and beating Asian women, would the courts have handled it differently? If his violence had targeted race, religion, or sexual orientation, would they have taken it more seriously? *Why not when the violence was clearly, consistently, and viciously aimed at women?*

Christen made them look at it through the right lens. She forced the question. And this time, someone actually fucking listened.

Darrell Meyer wasn't just another bureaucrat with a briefcase and a backlog—he was the first official to get genuinely, visibly pissed off on our behalf. He saw the mountain of evidence we'd collected—years of threats, beatings, and degrading, misogynistic filth—and decided enough was enough. He was done letting Jason terrorize women with no real consequences. *And damn, that felt good.*

Christen, Cassidy, and I were on high alert, ready to drive to Iowa at a moment's notice to testify. And Heather was already there waiting with bated breath. Oh, right—Cassidy. Remember the TU law student Jason stalked and harassed back in the '90s? Turns out she grew up to become a full-blown JAG officer—a government-trained legal badass who probably eats men like Jason for breakfast. And Heather—the Iowa nurse who once glared daggers at me in court—was also on tap, ready to testify. If the jury didn't believe me, Christen, or Heather, Miss JAG Officer Cassidy was our courtroom nuke. *Game over.*

Of course, nothing about Jason ever goes clean. In a twist that would've made Margaret Atwood cringe, Marci, who had nearly died from his attack, flipped the script. She ran right back to him. Just weeks after being hospitalized with life-threatening injuries, she started blaming the doctors for her condition. She claimed they hurt her, not Jason. That's how deep his manipulation runs. You could practically see the puppet strings from space.

And here's the thing—I wasn't even surprised that he convinced Marci to change her story. Because I *knew*. I knew how good he was at getting inside someone's head. At erasing logic and replacing it with fear. That's what Stockholm Syndrome does. It wraps around your mind like a vine and convinces you that the abuser is your lifeline instead of your threat. Jason didn't just abuse people physically—he dismantled them psychologically. He made them believe that survival meant loyalty. Hell, I had Stockholm Syndrome after just three weeks with him. So I can't even begin to fathom the level of mindfuck Marci endured. He didn't just get in her head—he set up camp, rewrote the rules, and made her question her own reality.

And it's more common than people think. Stockholm Syndrome isn't rare. It's real. It's what happens when someone breaks you down piece by piece and then convinces you they're the only one who can put you back together. Victims don't always know they're being abused. Even when they do, they might defend their abuser, or go back—because that's what trauma-bonding does.

So if you're reading this and any part of it feels a little too familiar—if you're with someone who's chipped away at your voice, your freedom, your fire—please know this: what you're feeling has a name. And it happens to the strongest people you know. It happens quietly, and then all at once. It happens to people who are smart, capable, strong, and full of fire. You're not broken. You're not alone. And you're not crazy.

Marci wasn't weak. Marci was being controlled. He had her finances. He was her boss. He grounded her from her phone like she was a teenager. Took her car keys. Controlled her medication. She had to hide pain meds from him like they were secrets that could get her punished. He isolated her from her family. She was cut off, shut down, and held under emotional lock and key. He knew exactly what he stood to lose if she ever exposed him. That's why he told her that if she spoke out, he'd kill her mom, her boys, and her. That wasn't a scare tactic. That was the trap.

The fact that she had the strength to call 911 from her Apple Watch that horrific night still quietly floors me.

This wasn't some storybook case of "why didn't she leave?" This was survival strategy. Psychological entrapment. The kind of control that doesn't leave bruises you can photograph—but leaves scars that can run your entire life.

Studies show that on average, it takes a woman *seven* times to leave an abuser for good. That doesn't make her weak. That makes the abuse *work*. It's designed to keep her stuck. But naming it is the first way out.

But we weren't going to let Marci's reversal derail the fight. Christen had been screaming for years that Jason's violence should be treated as a hate crime against women, and for the first time, someone finally saw it the way we did. Darrell got it. He understood that when someone attacks a person of color while shouting slurs, it's a hate crime—and when someone beats women while spewing gendered slurs and threats, *that's hate too.*

What's the nastiest word you can call a woman? A cunt. And Jason? He loved that word.

One of his greatest hits? "She's not a cunt like you, so no beatings required."

I still had that email saved from years ago. *I'll never delete it.*

Christen and I got to work. By then, I had leveled up my job and brought the skills with me. So, we built a full-blown interactive database, linked to a supporting spreadsheet. You know me—I color-coded it with all of my favorite colors. A fully sortable, clickable evidence log of every misogynistic insult he'd ever hurled—who he said it to, when, how, and in what context. We organized the vile. We archived the abuse. We made it searchable.

We called it The Cunt Database and provided it to the Hardin County Attorney's Office in Eldora, Iowa.

And to that we say: *fuck you, Jason.*

Right around the time Marci was fighting for her life and Jason was finally being charged like the predator he is, Christen channeled her inner real estate stalker and found his house on Zillow. We weren't even being nosy—we were just curious. After everything, who wouldn't look up the villain's lair?

She sent me the link, and I clicked. First photo: a tired-looking two-story house in Iowa, paint chipped, soul missing.

Second photo: the living room with sad furniture and bad lighting.

Third photo: the upstairs bathroom, with a haunting bottle of bleach placed by the toilet.

But by the fourth photo?

There it was.

The sign.

The same one he printed with my face on it—the one he used to plaster around Sapulpa back in 2017, the one a judge reprimanded him for in open court. That sign was now in his fucking yard. In Iowa. On Zillow. Four years later, three states away, 523 miles from where it started—and he brought it with him like it was some cherished family heirloom.

And it gets even creepier. He didn't just bring it to Iowa and stick it in the yard—he had it displayed *inside* the house too. Hung on the wall like fine art. And in one of his posts online, there she was—his new wife—posing in front of it inside the house. *My face looming behind her in the photo like some twisted, permanent houseguest.*

It was like a hate crime and a real estate listing had a baby.

This man—this monster—once tried to convince a courtroom that *I* was obsessed with *him.* That was his story. That I was unstable, couldn't let go, and was ruining his life because I couldn't handle rejection. *Meanwhile, he literally moved across the country and brought his creepy-ass sign with him like it was a framed family portrait.* Projection, party of one.

But here's the thing: at this point? *Fucking eh right I'm obsessed with him.* I'm obsessed with holding his ass accountable. With making sure every woman he tries to charm, groom, gaslight, or destroy knows exactly who he is. *I'm obsessed with making damn sure his reign of terror ends.*

He wasn't even trying to hide it. This wasn't buried in the background—it was front and center. *"Come tour this charming colonial featuring a basement, updated kitchen, and casual terrorism!"* I stared at it, dumbfounded. Then I laughed. Not because it was funny—but because *if I didn't, I'd scream. Throw my laptop. Or both.* Who the hell sees a photo like that and thinks, *"Oh yes, this seems like a safe neighborhood"*? Zillow should've flagged it under psychological warfare.

It was just another reminder: Jason never let go of his hatred. He nurtured it like a houseplant.

As the trial in Eldora, Iowa loomed, depositions were scheduled for each of us: me, Christen, Heather, and Cassidy. We weren't together. Each of us had our own time, our own screen, our own setting. Heather gave hers from home in Iowa. Christen's was first—just the way the schedule shook out. Cassidy's, though, was a secret weapon. She hadn't stayed in touch with any of us. She wasn't part of the Unicorn Club, hadn't compared stories. Her testimony came from a completely independent place, which made it airtight. No one could accuse her of bias or collusion. She was a decorated JAG officer with a calm, measured delivery, and her credibility made her story hit like a freight train.

When it was my turn, I had one request: I wanted Taylor Burke beside me. He offered, and I said hell yes. His downtown Tulsa office was a cathedral of credibility—glass-walled, espresso-scented, fancy in a way that screamed, *People win cases here.* And on that day, I felt like I had fucking earned my place in a room like that.

I wore a blazer jacket over a t-shirt that said *"Sweep the Leg,"* masked up because it was still the pandemic. The shirt stayed completely covered—no one saw it—but I knew it was under there. *It was my own secret, my own reminder that I'm here to fight and win.* I sat in the glossy boardroom with my coffee and my notes, facing a screen that fed straight into a law office hundreds of miles away. No glares, no judge, no Jason staring daggers across the aisle. Just me, Taylor, and the truth.

Well—me, Taylor, and Jason's attorney, who appeared onscreen to question me. Jason wasn't visible—he was too chickenshit to face me—but it was obvious he was there. His attorney kept glancing to the side, clearly consulting someone off-camera. *You didn't need a detective badge to figure out who.*

And here's the thing: I felt a strange wave of relief when I realized I'd be questioned by her—the wife half of that CNN-highlighted husband-and-wife legal duo, famous for defending high-profile murder suspects, including the guy who famously murdered Mollie Tibbetts. After years of being shut down and belittled by male attorneys, it was almost a gift to finally face a woman. I'm not saying all men are assholes, but let's be real—most of the ones I'd faced across courtrooms absolutely were.

And I used every second of it.

I was poised. I was well-spoken. I had been waiting years to say these words. This wasn't the girl Jason had hurt. This was the woman who'd graduated *summa cum laude* from Hell University, and I was ready to start taking names out of the handbasket I had brought back with me.

I laid it all out—the threats, the beatings, the signs, the court enforced silence. I walked them through the flyer. Through the years of fear. I watched her face twist in surprise when I brought up my little ugly masterpiece—the one Jason never thought would resurface. She had no idea it existed. She was sitting there, trying to paint Jason as a man who had never hurt a woman, who had no pattern of misogyny or abuse.

And I dropped a bomb: I'd been calling him a serial abuser for years. I had printed proof.

The moment I mentioned the flyer, she froze. Then, with a forced smile, she asked to take a brief break to consult with her client.

I smirked. That little detour? That was the sound of her game plan unraveling in real time.

And I addressed the lie that always made my skin crawl: that I was obsessed with Jason. That I was some desperate, delusional ex. But let's be honest—who's the one who made a sign with my face on it and kept it in his yard three states away for four damn years?

And like I said before, *fucking right I was obsessed.* Obsessed with making sure he never hurt another woman again.

I wasn't just going into that sworn deposition with the flyer as my ace in the hole. I also had the news Heather had reluctantly recently confessed to me, because she knew I would eventually find out. The moment that will stay with me forever. During her deposition earlier that week, Heather—the same Heather who once glared at me across a courtroom—swore under oath that Jason had been plotting to murder me at the Tulsa State Fair. Not just some vague, empty threat. An actual plan. The kind that creeps into your spine and stays there. He wanted me dead. And he had picked a time, a place, and a method.

All those years I'd been dismissed as dramatic, unstable, exaggerating? They shattered in that instant. *The danger had been real. The fear had been earned. My instincts hadn't lied. I hadn't been overreacting.*

So when Jason's attorney started her long string of "gotcha" questioning that morning, I didn't blink. I met her questions head-on, steady and calm.

And when my deposition came to an end, I leaned back in that leather chair, took a sip of coffee, and it was then I realized:

He never shut me up.

Jason's chances of beating these eight charges were slim, and his attorneys knew it. Instead of facing life in prison, Jason took a plea deal and pled guilty to Willful Injury Causing Serious Injury and was sentenced to ten years in a state penitentiary that specializes in rehabilitating sexual predators. And Marci? She made it out. She survived him. And whether or not the system understood it, *we* did. When it mattered most, she saved her own life. The forced separation from her abuser offered Marci the clarity she needed to finally start seeing through the manipulation. Marci and Jason were soon divorced, and she was issued her immediate membership card to our little tribe we never asked to be in. She is in the Unicorn Club now too, and she's one of the strongest women I have ever met.

We were told he'd get life for what he did to Marci. We dared to hope. We needed that hope. Ten years didn't feel like enough, but it was something. Enough time for her to start healing, for the rest of us to exhale—for a small fraction of justice to settle in.

But Jason Lewis doesn't stay caged.

After just thirteen months—*thirteen months*—he walked out of prison early. Why? *"Good behavior." Puke.*

We didn't even have time to relocate. No heads-up. No warning. Just boom—he's out. Wearing an ankle monitor like a Fitbit, strolling back into the world like the system didn't just witness the carnage he caused.

He did less time than Martha Stewart did for insider trading.

Read that again.

A man who nearly murdered his wife served less time than a woman who lied about stocks.

We thought the nightmare was over. Instead, the system handed him the key and said, *"Have a nice life."*

But here's the difference now—he's being watched. Closely. By the state. By parole officers.

And by us.

Because I'll never stop exposing the monster who raped me. *And he fucking knows it.* He might be out of prison and tucked into the comfort of his own bed—but he will never again enjoy the comfort of my silence.

After the Iowa Parole Board released Jason from prison—not after "life," as we were promised, but after just a few months—they dumped him back into the world without notifying any of the women he had terrorized. Not even Marci, the one he'd just served time for.

So yeah, we threw a fit. A big one. Me, Christen, Heather, and Marci raised hell through gritted teeth and frustrated tears. We weren't asking for special treatment—we were begging for basic safety. We were given zero notice that the monster would be released, no time to move where he couldn't find us. That collective fury led to the Iowa Parole Board creating something they called a "Victim's Roundtable," which sounds very formal but was basically a group Zoom call where all four of us were invited to express our concerns... with a police officer from each of our hometowns on the line.

Enter: Sapulpa Police Captain Mike Sole.

I'll never forget watching him sit there, forced to hear in real time what the long-term consequences of his department's inaction looked like. That man got a crash course in "this is what happens when you phone it in." At the end of the meeting, I was told to save his number—he would be my new point of contact. The one officer in Sapulpa PD who would finally take my safety seriously. And for a minute, it felt like a small win. I thought, *Okay, maybe we've finally got someone in a Sapulpa Police Uniform who cares about me.*

Cut to a few months later: the Iowa Parole Board's inmate information notification system *lost track* of Jason Lewis. I don't mean he slipped through the cracks—I mean, they literally had no clue where a convicted sex offender with a violent history had gone, according to the alert. And given the horror movie that is my life, I genuinely thought he might be coming for me.

So I did what I was told to do. I called Captain Mike Sole. Left a voicemail. A clear one. Scared. Vulnerable. Waiting.

He never called me back.

And just like that, my tiny spark of hometown hope fizzled out. I guess expecting my local police department to care was adorable of me.

Luckily the alert was just a glitch and Jason Lewis was in Iowa where he was supposed to be, and my fear was unwarranted.

Chapter Seventeen

The Podcast

"I can feel it in the future, I can see it in the culture." — Wilderado, "Surefire"

If you'd told me back when I was teaching piano in my tiny studio that one of my students would go on to be the director of a legal justice center—and then use her platform to tell *my* story—I would've laughed. Not because I didn't believe in her. But because, let's face it, at that point, *I couldn't see anyone believing in me.*

Colleen McCarty first walked into my life as a woman on a mission: she was learning a piano piece to surprise her husband, and I was all in. We pulled off the full rom-com setup—champagne, candles, strawberries—and I secretly recorded a video of the moment. Years later, she'd pull off something even more incredible: dedicating an entire season of her podcast to exposing the man who tried to destroy me.

After years of legal work and rising through the ranks, Colleen became the Executive Director of the Oklahoma Appleseed Center for Law and Justice. She and Leslie Briggs, also an attorney, co-hosted *Panic Button*, a podcast originally dedicated to the case of April Wilkens—a woman who killed her rapist and has spent decades in prison for it.

April's story is devastating and unforgettable. She's the reason Panic Button exists in the first place, and I'm forever grateful to her in more ways than she'll ever know. April, if you're reading this—your story has brought out the activist in me, and you're the strongest woman in this whole book. *God I hope you're reading this in the comfort of your home.*

When Colleen found out that Jason got out of prison in only thirteen months, she didn't just get mad—she got moving. She decided Season 2 would be about him. About me. About us.

They called it *Panic Button: Season 2 – Operation Wildfire.*

When Colleen told me, I just stood there—equal parts floored, frozen, and grateful. Out of all the injustices in the state of Oklahoma—and that's a long-ass list—they chose mine. I knew it would stir things up. I also knew *it was time.* Being chosen meant my voice, and the voices of the other women Jason had hurt, would finally echo far beyond the four walls of a courthouse.

We recorded at a cool little studio in an office park called Wompa—full podcast setup, comfy couch, headphones and fancy microphones that made you feel like your voice mattered. I sat across from Colleen and Leslie, with a couple of legal interns sitting nearby who had clearly researched Jason like their lives depended on it. *I don't think I've ever seen anyone hang on my every word like that.* It wasn't just an interview. *It was a goddamn exorcism.*

The first episode kicked off with a voice I didn't expect to hear so soon—Heather's. The podcaster introduced her, "That was Heather. She was married to Jason when he was embroiled in a defamation suit against a woman who claimed he was a serial abuser." That woman? Me. They weren't tiptoeing. They were diving straight into the deep end of my crazy story with that opening line.

Then the voiceover came in: *"If the monster that hurt you was still out there, how far would you go to warn others? And what would you do if the justice system was no longer on your side?"*

Holy shit. They were talking about me. And I knew the answer. *I had already gone as far as you can go without setting the world on fire.*

I wasn't the only one with a story to tell. The podcast opened the floodgates—voices poured in, some familiar, some long buried in the shadows. Women I knew. Women I didn't. All of us tangled in the same web spun by a man who should've been locked away for life.

Episode after episode peeled back layer after grotesque layer. One of the early stories came from Cassidy, the one with the forever protective order, the TU Law student Jason dated in the late '90s. She met him online in 1997. One night, after a fight, he slammed her head into the windshield of her car, choked her, and stole her keys so she couldn't leave. Then he took her home. She survived, barely. Her attorney at the time told her to hang onto every document because, someday, she might get a call to testify in a murder trial.

Cassidy stayed. Jason promised therapy, AA meetings. They even moved in together.

Eventually, she got a protective order. It took until 1998.

Then came the deep dive into Jason's family—starting with Jason Lewis Sr., a man who makes your skin crawl just hearing his name. Jason's dad was in and out of prison (mostly in), and even more slippery than his son. Among the greatest hits? Stealing semis full of meat from the mafia. And then moonlighting—brace yourself—as an unlicensed gynecologist in Denver. *That is not satire.* This man offered gynecological care with the same qualifications it takes to run a hot dog stand.

Jason once told Cassidy he watched his father abuse his mother. He told Christen the same. Told Heather, too. Jason Sr., of course, denied it all. But the pattern was there—generation after generation of violence wrapped in charm.

And then—Josh Kidd.

Hearing Jason's former attorney on the podcast was such a pleasant surprise. This was the same guy who once dragged me through court like I was the villain. Jason's business partner. His legal bulldog. And here he was, on tape, telling the truth. He said, "Jason's mother defended him to the death, she believed he was innocent of everything."

I waited for the dig at me. *It never came.*

What did come? A moment I never thought I'd hear in my lifetime: Josh Kidd admitting Jason was not the man he once believed him to be. But just hearing confirmation that the Good Ole Boy Network had been busted was righteous.

Then came Catey.

Jason's sister. The one who died by suicide. At least, that's what they say. *I've always assumed otherwise.* Jason bragged about writing her epitaph. When Colleen and Leslie visited her grave, they read it aloud:

"All the pain and grief are over, every restless tossing passed, I am now at peace forever, I am safely home at last."

He was proud of that.

And through all this, the hosts kept pulling back the curtain on the system. The statistics were staggering. Oklahoma—ranked second in the nation for women killed by men. Twenty people a minute are assaulted by intimate partners in this country. Jason had beaten multiple women with the same dowel rod. Branded them. Punched us while driving. Sewed Marci's scalp shut without anesthesia to avoid a hospital visit. And he still got out of prison in thirteen months. Wearing an ankle monitor. With no warning. No heads-up. Just *poof*—paroled.

The system had failed Marci. It had failed all of us.

There was this rhythm to *Panic Button*—just when you thought it couldn't get darker, it did. As Christen's story unfolded, and even though I already knew it by heart, hearing it told through the polished narration of a podcast made it feel even more cinematic.

After Jason stole her truck, Christen called the cops, but they told her since she knew who had the truck, it wasn't technically stolen. She didn't cry. She loaded her daughter in the car (she needed a driver), grabbed her pistol, and drove straight to Sharon's trailer park. The truck was there. Keys still in it. Jason, somewhere inside, probably passed out in the wreckage of his own life.

Without flinching, Christen got her truck back. No drama. Just justice, DIY-style. *That's my best friend, folks.*

But even her story didn't prepare listeners for what came next.

Jason's time working at the funeral home had always been one of those facts we tried not to think about too hard. The podcast made sure we did think about it. Wouldn't you know it? Later, Trisha came around too. She ended up speaking on the podcast, finally confirming exactly who Jason really was. She shared how he used to brag to her that he had sex with dead bodies while he worked as a mortician. Not once. Not as a joke. Repeatedly. Casually. The same woman who once called me a *"psycho crazy bitch"* was now adding her voice to the chorus. *Eventually, most everyone who hated me in the beginning comes around . Truth has a way of working like that.*

He said he used to wonder what it would be like. Claimed he had those thoughts while embalming a corpse. Heather added that he used to say, if he wanted to be sweet, he'd tie a bow around a dead man's penis before burial—like it was his version of tenderness. He constantly insisted that he'd *"never have sex with a dead body."* And honestly, *the more someone denies something that loudly and that often, the harder it is to believe them.*

Heather finally put it together after comparing notes with me and Christen. *"I always thought that was odd,"* she said on the podcast, *"because why would you even bring that up?"*

Another pattern emerged, thanks to Maggie. Jason had used the legal system like a weapon during their divorce. He threatened her with jail. Filed motion after motion. Played legal chicken with her sanity. Leslie, the co-host, nailed it: "This theme of abusing the court process—not in pursuit of any kind of justice but to harm his former partners—that's going to come up again, and again, and again throughout this podcast."

Yeah, no shit.

He weaponized power. Any kind of power. If he could file it, fake it, forge it, or fight with it, he would.

After 8 weekly episodes of pure vindication through shared stories of our shared abuser, then came the moment I had been waiting for. It wasn't even in the podcast yet. It was on my kitchen Alexa.

Every week, it would show the upcoming episode's title card before the newest episode dropped at midnight. Just the cover. No sound. No content. Just a little image and a title card to tease what was coming next.

And that morning, there it was. The words *"Panic Button Season 2: Operation Wildfire – Episode 9 – Wildfire."* And under that...

My flyer.

The one he had tried so hard to destroy. The one he sued me over. The one I designed with shaky hands and printed at Christen's office like we were running an underground resistance—because in a way, we were. The one we plastered on cork boards, taped to storefronts, and tacked to telephone poles all across his hometown. The one that warned other women he was a serial abuser. The one that got my First Amendment rights stripped for 441 days straight.

And now it was glowing—clear as day—on my kitchen Alexa screen. Right next to the coffee pot. Right next to my cookbooks. The same flyer that nearly ruined my life... was now part of a podcast that was making sense of it.

He tried to bury it. *The world dug it up.*

🔥

When the "Wildfire" episode was released, it began:

> *"Everything in life has a tipping point. No matter what, at some point, the way you've been living becomes too much, and something has to give. For Jason Lewis, that tipping point came when he met Karrah. He didn't know that was the moment—and neither did she. But the end of their relationship sparked a series of events almost too crazy to believe."*

That was the first thing you heard in Episode 9.

That's when I knew.

I sat there, AirPods in, heart pounding, and thought: *Holy shit—they said it. They literally credited me with sparking the beginning of the end of this man's reign of terror.*

And I'll take it.

Because I fought fucking hard. And long. And loud. And consistently. I earned the right to hold that line like a trophy I carved out of court filings and trauma and sheer goddamn willpower. I didn't get there by being the perfect victim. I got there by refusing to shut up.

The *Wildfire* episode was the first time I got to tell that story publicly. Really tell it. Not in court, where everything I said was cross-examined to death. Not behind closed doors. Not in conversations that felt like whispered confessions. This was the full story, told to the world.

I got to talk about designing the flyer. Printing it secretly at Christen's office. Driving to his hometown in the white Mustang with the flyers on the dash and a knot in my stomach. Naming the car *Wildfire*, because the truth was going to spread no matter what.

The eight harrowing episodes leading up to mine had already done the groundwork—each claim in our flyer had been independently confirmed by survivor testimony, court records, timelines, receipts. By the time *Wildfire* aired, it wasn't speculation. It was truth, fully substantiated. Episode 9 wasn't a "reveal"—it was the moment all the puzzle pieces snapped together.

There were parts of the episode that were hard to hear. One in particular—when they questioned why I hadn't secured legal representation sooner. That part hurt. Not because they were wrong, but because I had tried so hard. *If they had known how many dead ends I ran into, how many lawyers ghosted me, how many said it was too risky to represent someone being sued for calling her abuser exactly what he was—I think that moment would've landed differently.* I wasn't careless. I was desperate.

Still, nothing could touch the way it felt to hear my own words, my own war story, finally broadcast back to me in a format that gave it weight.

I sat at my kitchen table, coffee cooling beside me, and just listened. My Alexa screen still showed the flyer—the one Jason tried to bury—and my AirPods whispered the fire back into my chest. Toward the end of the episode, they asked Josh Kidd what he thought of Jason Lewis these days.

> *"I think everything you need to know about Jason, you can talk to Karrah Youngblood and the alleged victims. I have a lot of respect for her, even though she probably doesn't respect me at all, I have a lot of respect for Karrah, especially now that we know that Jason is an abuser."*

That's powerful shit right there, y'all.

All I could think about was that line I smugly delivered to him all those years ago in that courthouse hallway. *"You're gonna like me one day, Josh."*

Episode 10 was called *Eureka!*—and the second I saw that title drop, my stomach flipped. I knew exactly where this was going.

Jason had always sworn—under oath, on the record—that he never hurt anyone in Arkansas. Lied right through his teeth, like always. And now the podcast was about to call his bluff in the loudest, most public way possible—with the voice of a woman named Carisa.

None of us had ever met her. Not me, not Christen, not Heather, not Marci. She wasn't some part of our survivor circle. She wasn't a voice we found through advocacy groups or mutual friends. She was out there completely on her own, for decades, carrying this nightmare silently. She had no idea there was even a list of women like her.

But let's give credit where credit is due—this didn't just happen by accident. The team at Appleseed had been trying to locate Carisa for months with no success. And then Christen, being Christen, pulled out her Google search magic and found her. She tracked her down when the legal researchers couldn't, and once Appleseed finally connected with her, Carisa agreed to speak. And that was the first time her story finally entered this hellish puzzle.

Carisa had never told her story publicly before, other than that time she peeked her head out to make the comment on Channel 6's website. She'd only told two people: her mother—and the Eureka Springs Police Department.

She met Jason in 1997. Same charming routine. Same polished lies. And then one morning, she knocked on the door of a hotel room, and something in her gut screamed: *Don't go in.*

She went in anyway.

What happened inside that room was horrifying. He bit her. He yanked her lip until it bled. He shoved his fingers down her throat to stop her from screaming. He beat her with a belt. He told her that no one knew where she was, that no one was coming, that her body would never be found. *It was word-for-word the same horror show we all lived in our own versions—but she didn't even know how eerily her story mirrored ours.*

Carisa managed to escape that room and staggered into the hotel lobby, hysterical. The police were called. A report was filed. Jason was arrested for domestic battery. And just like that, her name was quietly added to the list—the list she didn't even know existed.

She spoke like it had happened yesterday. Her voice was steady, even as she described how his entire fist fit inside her mouth. How she had to pay for a taxi to get back to Tulsa. How she never saw him again. And how utterly shocked she was to learn that, all these years later, Jason still wasn't in prison for life—or worse.

"I'm surprised he's not wanted for murder," she said. *"Because there's nothing in his soul."*

And the thing that made her story so powerful was that she wasn't corroborating ours—she was *confirming* it. Carisa didn't know us.

We had never exchanged a single word. But every single horrifying detail aligned perfectly with the experiences we'd spent years screaming into the void. The same abuse. The same language. The same patterns.

For all the times we were told that women standing together made us less credible—Carisa proved exactly the opposite.

And at the end of her interview, she said something I'll never forget. Reflecting on how much stronger she was now, Carisa said that if Jason tried to hurt her today, she'd be out there in the streets holding signs with his name on them.

I got chills.

Because what she didn't know—what she couldn't have known—was that I already had.

After the podcast came to a conclusion, the messages started. Not from reporters. Not from media outlets. From survivors.

Women I'd never met. Women I'll probably never meet. Some sent a single sentence. Some wrote paragraphs. Some just sent a heart. But the meaning was always the same: *"Damn you're brave."* And that—that meant everything.

Because for so long, I was treated like I'd lit a match just to watch the world burn. Like the flyer was some dramatic cry for attention. Like I was unstable, vengeful, out for blood. But now, people were seeing what it really was: a warning. A record. A lifeline. *The thing that finally said, stop fucking hurting women, or else.*

Carisa's story sealed it. She never saw the flyer, never compared notes with another survivor. And still—her account mirrored ours like it had been pulled from the same nightmare. That kind of truth doesn't need a fact-check. It just *lands.* And when it did, something shifted. People didn't ask for proof. They didn't demand we explain ourselves. *They just listened.*

And the podcast didn't stop there. After *Eureka*, they kept going—devoting an entire episode to Marci's story. It was hard to hear. Her injuries. The dowel rod. The branding. The trauma she endured behind closed doors. But it was important. Because it showed, in no uncertain terms, that Jason didn't stop after me. Or Christen. Or Heather. Or Carisa. *He just kept going until the state finally did something. And even then, it wasn't enough.*

The flyer, once used to paint me as unhinged, had now been carefully described to thousands of people. Understood. Respected. It was no longer something I had to defend. *It was evidence of what happens when a woman gets tired of being quiet.*

And as the comments kept coming, I realized something simple but life-changing:

Everyone believes me now.

I'll never be able to thank the Oklahoma Appleseed Center for Law and Justice enough. They didn't just help me tell my story—they gave it weight. Legal weight. Emotional weight. The kind of weight that says, *"We see you. We believe you. And we're going to do something about it."* After years of being told to shut up, settle down, or let it go, they handed me a goddamn megaphone and said, *"Go ahead, let it burn."* Being chosen as their season wasn't just an honor—it was the first time I felt like my name came with power instead of shame. Listeners tuned in from Germany, Sweden, Australia—places I've never been but where my truth somehow landed.

The fire had finally caught. The Wildfire was spreading.

Chapter Eighteen

The Last Word.

"I know every mile will be worth my while." —Peyton Parrish, "Go the Distance"

Even after the podcast, Jason was still out there being Jason—still finding ways to take his shots at me online. During all of this, when the Iowa Parole Board finally forced him off of social media, it wasn't because he voluntarily stayed quiet. Before they shut him down, he was still out there mocking me under an alias, "Jamie Looney." Saying I lived in my dad's basement. Saying no one believes my bullshit. Of course, the drugs I am so heavily addicted to.

In response to my post asking why sexual predators are allowed to have Instagram, he posted a screenshot of some obscure legal statute about how even sex offenders had First Amendment rights to social media—conveniently leaving out that his parole orders explicitly forbid him from using it. And attached to that? A classy little public post that started with:

"Hey Pumpkin."

Hey Pumpkin! While you're out playing vigilante, spreading lies, slandering and making your COUNTLESS false claims, at least take the time to fact check your bullshit. As usual, you're wrong. Crazy ass, lying trash.

And then came the hashtags—like some delusional highlight reel:

#youretheproblem #noonebelievesyou #youre-aliar #stalker #obsessedwithlies #attentionwhore #noonecares #youhavenolikes #failure #seethroughthe-bullshit #moveon

That "#youhavenolikes" jab was classic Jason. As if the number of likes determined whether I had value. The irony? A few weeks later, I started casually posting my pumpkin carvings on TikTok and Instagram—and in one month, I crossed one million likes. Over 30 million views across platforms that October. I even landed a brand deal with a major cosmetics company—NYX Cosmetics brought me on for their Halloween social media push, commissioning a custom jack-o'-lantern carved with their logo. And when NPR's *Morning Edition*—the most listened-to radio show in the country—featured my creations in a national story? That felt like a high five from the universe.

Turns out, people like my art. And Jason? He can choke on his hashtags.

So let's talk about Carisa.

The girl Jason Lewis swore didn't exist. The one he beat in Arkansas. The one I listed on my flyer—*his* flyer—that he lied about under oath in a courtroom, trying to erase her like she was just another bad dream. For years, she stayed quiet. And honestly—who could blame her? She was only nineteen when he tore her world apart in a hotel room in Eureka Springs, Arkansas and then carried on like nothing happened. She ran. Disappeared. Probably the smartest fucking move any of us made.

I always thought she was brave for that. Brave for getting out. Brave for not looking back. And I never stopped thinking about her.

So when I heard her voice on the podcast—her voice, telling her story—I cried big honkin' tears. They dedicated an entire episode to what that bastard did to her in 1997, and it hit like a wave of *holy shit* and *hallelujah.* Still, even after speaking her truth into the mic, she wasn't ready to join me and Christen and our silly little support club—and again, I don't blame her. She didn't owe us a damn thing.

Then one beautiful Oklahoma spring day in 2025, it happened. Out of nowhere, Carisa messaged me back. After years of me dropping little notes in her inbox—tiny reminders that she was *my goddamn hero*—she finally opened one.

At first, she was guarded. She hadn't even listened to the podcast she was on—said it tore open too many wounds. But something about our exchange started to shift things. Our texting turned into a phone call, and she learned that Jason wasn't a one-time monster but a full-blown, serial predator who had never stopped hurting women. When she saw how hard I'd been working with the other survivors to hold him accountable, I could feel it happen—*click*—that same spark I'd felt light up in myself, Christen, Heather, Marci...

"I'll help in any way I can," she said.

So I put her in touch with the documentary film crew.

You heard me. There's a documentary.

Turns out some talented young filmmakers in New York got wind of this story—and built an entire production company just to turn this crazy tale into a film. Yeah. Wild.

They've been to Iowa twice to film Heather. They've been to Oklahoma twice to film me, Christen, and Marci. They followed us around with a full film crew when we were marching at the State Capitol. At one point, they even rented a slick-ass Mustang, crammed a sound guy and a cameraman into the backseat, and followed us around Sapulpa with a drone like we were making a goddamn Netflix crime series. They recreated my flyer. They filmed Christen and me hanging it. They shot me standing in front of the courthouse, flipping off the police station (*because of course I did*).

They captured Christen in her real estate office. They filmed Marci in a law office. They filmed me inside Saied Music, where I once taught piano lessons in between dodging Jason's punches. They even filmed me inside the recital hall—where I used to showcase my students—except this time, I was sitting in front of a camera crew, answering a sweet producer's endless stream of questions and telling my story to a very expensive-looking camera. Full fucking circle.

And then—once Heather made it down from Iowa to join us—they packed us all back into that Mustang and followed us with the drone again while we drove together down Boston Pool Road. The same road where he'd beaten so many women. There was something cathartic about that. Taking those backroads—on our own terms. Together. Alive.

But nothing hit me harder than when they interviewed my daughter. Rayne sat there, calm and clear, and told them she never knew any of this was happening when she was growing up. That I had shielded her from it completely. That I was her hero.

Fuck. That was the win.

And when Carisa learned there was an independent film being made, she lit up at the chance to finally say it out loud to a camera: *Fuck you, Jason.* Her words. Her truth. Her moment.

What makes her story so powerful—so undeniably important—is that, like Cassidy, she didn't know the rest of us. She hadn't been inducted into our unofficial survivors' circle. We didn't trade stories. We didn't compare scars. She instantaneously validated all of our pain without even knowing it.

Carisa is proof this didn't start in 2014 with me. She's proof this didn't start with Christen. Or with Sharon, Maggie, or Keely, Cassidy, or Brittany, Heather, Marci, etc. He's been brutalizing women since at least the goddamn '90s.

Talking to Carisa reminded me why I've stayed in this fight for ten fucking years. Why I never stopped. Why I'll never stop. Carisa coming back into the light felt like the universe handing me a tiny gold medal. Proof that using my voice still matters. That survivors like her—like *us*—are never alone.

Before we hung up, Carisa said something that hit like a freight train made of grace.

She thanked me.

She told me that what I'd done—standing up to him when no one else could or would—gave her a voice. That I had saved lives. She called me a real hero for getting under his skin like I have. She said the scared, beaten girl from all those years ago thanks me for standing up to her bully. And that the woman she is today? She thanks me, too.

I wasn't prepared for how hard that would hit. Because I've spent a decade shouting into the abyss, wondering if anything I did would ever matter. Wondering if anyone heard me. If anyone believed me. If the price I paid to speak was worth a damn thing.

But in that moment, hearing those words from the ever-elusive Arkansas survivor, I realized something deep in my bones: *it was worth it. It is worth it. It will always be worth it.*

And I told her, *"Well... the little girl in me thanks me, too."*

And she does.

Because for the first time in a long time, I felt like she would be proud of me. Because I sleep well every night knowing I stood up to one of the most documented, vicious predators in modern history.

Me.

Artsy-fartsy, flighty, dancing in my kitchen, Pink Floyd lovin', goofy, smart-ass me.

And I didn't just survive it.

I burned the motherfucker's playbook.

These days, I run my own graphic design firm—a space where I don't have to answer to men, or be talked down to in meetings, or ask permission to be brilliant. Dr. Baird and Saied Music Company remain two of my most loyal clients. *Never burn bridges, folks!* I design posters, build websites, run high-level campaigns, and can design a real sexy QR code, if I do say so myself. I tell stories through visuals. I design things that stick. My job is to make people feel something—and I'm good at it. I build beauty from scratch. I create meaning with typography. And soon, I'll be teaching Adult Beginner Piano again. I was recently hired by the Paycom Center to carve a custom Jack O'Lantern *for the Oklahoma City Thunder themselves*—this year's NBA Finals Champs—for their opening game this fall. No big deal... just my art courtside.

I alchemize pain into purpose every damn day. *And I'm not alone.*

Christen and I? We've become full-blown advocates—marching at the Oklahoma State Capitol, petitioning lawmakers to help pass the Oklahoma Survivors Act. Christen even used her real estate knowledge to launch an LLC called "Firestorm Land Group," buying land and homes to turn into shelters for battered women. (*I designed her logo—obviously.*)

We show up. We speak out. And sometimes, Marci does too. She's back in healthcare, living in her own place, holding it down like a boss. She plans to use her voice to tell her story and advocate for women being believed the first damn time. She recently told me, "If I can help even one person who is being abused, then I feel like every bit of what I've been through was worth it." *Like I said before, she's one of the strongest people I know.*

Heather's still up in Iowa, is now a Nurse Practitioner and is married to The County Sheriff with a police dog trained to eat intruders on command—so she sleeps just fine.

And Josh Kidd? He dropped Jason as a client right around the time Taylor Burke entered the picture. He moved to California with his lovely family, is a content creator, and is somehow one of my favorite people in the world. We plan on starting up a podcast together one day. He quit practicing law after my defamation case because he felt the legal system was too corrupt. *You're welcome, Josh. I did that.*

Carisa? She's thriving in Oregon. A traveling registered nurse and flipping houses solo like a goddamn beast.

Me? I'm still raising a teenager, caring for my handicapped dad full-time, and making art every day for money. I wear a smaller size these days, but honestly? The peace I have in my heart fits better than any pair of jeans ever has.

Christen? Still the person who picks up on the first ring. Still my ride or die.

We're not just surviving anymore. *We're fucking happy.*

We have each other. And we're still here.

Christen recently sent me a simple little note that said: "*Karrah, I'm so glad you won. I'm so glad you pushed and pushed to hold on to the best parts of you.*"

She gives me the credit, but no, Christen—thank you.

If Jason hadn't hurt her, I wouldn't have found my way into this fight at all.

I wasn't strong enough to stand up for myself back then, but something in me had the balls to stand up for *her.*

After all is said and done, I am deeply grateful to have met Jason Lewis. If not for him, I may have never realized the kind of strength that was always simmering inside me. He didn't break me—he revealed me. And for that, I'm oddly thankful.

I realize now that it was never my shame to carry for being hurt. It was Jason's the whole time. And while he may not be in prison at the time of publishing, he's stuck being Jason Lewis. The Mortician, the fake Pilot, the fake Lawyer, the "Entrepreneur," the Personal Injury Consultant, Professional Victim, etc.

And honestly? That's a sentence all its own.

He can't use social media the way he used to. He can't publicly bully me without his pulpit. He can't flirt his way out of who he really is anymore. No lies, no new victims, no reinvention. Just him—rotting in the truth he created. Miserable. Bitter. Alone. The predator who finally ran out of prey.

Women can see him now for what he truly is. And I will forever hold my head high—knowing I boldly warned future victims. Knowing I told my story while forming lifelong friendships along the way. Knowing he only changed me for the better. Knowing I told my truth without ever backing down...

...and the truth will never stop burning.

O₂

Chapter Nineteen

Be the Oxygen

"So let's start a fire." —P!nk, "I Am Here"

I'm telling this story now because it felt like the obvious thing to do after someone went to such drastic measures to stop me from doing so. But you made it here. You stayed. You listened. And that means everything to me.

If this memoir lit even a small fire in you, please don't keep it to yourself. Share it with someone who's still hiding their hurt. Share it with someone who needs to know it was never their shame to carry. Share it with someone who's still afraid to speak. Share it with anyone who needs to learn from one of my countless mistakes. Share it with someone who needs a reminder of how strong they are.

And if you believe the truth should be louder than the people who try to silence it, then stand with me. Stand with me so the next girl doesn't have to walk through hell just to be heard. Stand with me so no survivor ever feels like they have to go through this alone.

Stand with me so the spark we lit doesn't just survive—it spreads. Quietly at first. A whisper here. A conversation there. A brave share. A repost. A moment of "me too" in someone else's inbox. And then louder. Brighter. Stronger. Because that's how wildfires start—not with a roar, but with a single, stubborn flame that refuses to go out.

Sharing my story is the only true justice I will ever receive.

So please help me carry this. Help me keep it alive. May it forever spread like… *well, you know.*

Chapter Twenty

"Karrah, Don't Sing"

"Just an earth-bound misfit, I." —Pink Floyd, "Learning to Fly"

Let's end this thing the way I began: **loud.** *Because I didn't become mouthy overnight. I was raised loud. Raised curious. Raised to speak up—even when it made people uncomfortable. Raised to say the kind of shit that made people squirm, then laugh, then think.*

Look, I know some of you might not give a damn about my magical, chaotic, loud-ass childhood—and that's fine. No offense taken. But if you've ever wondered how someone ends up with a mouth that refuses to stay shut—even when a judge tells her to—this chapter might give you some clues.

This is the origin story. The messy, musical, mischievous backstory that shaped the piano-teaching, pumpkin-carving, shit-talking loud-mouth you just spent a whole book with.

This is where I came from. And I wouldn't change a damn thing.

My mouth has always gotten me in trouble. I have never meant to be rude, but I have always had a lot to say and was a product of an environment where I was encouraged to do so. I'm pretty sure there were notes sent home (and worse) from every teacher that was ever lucky enough to be graced with my incessant need to ask questions. I wouldn't just ask for answers for myself, but I would ask the questions the other kids were afraid to ask. I learned early on that if I got straight A's, my mamma wouldn't gripe at me too much for the progress reports highlighting my "unsatisfactory" talking grade. My mother often told the story that I spoke in full sentences before my first birthday, and I haven't stopped using my voice ever since.

Most people close to me don't even call me Karrah. I go by KJ to just about everyone who really knows me. I've picked up a few other nicknames along the way too—like Junebug, from when I was little and absolutely mortified of those crunchy little bastards dive-bombing my hair every summer. And then there was "Karl"—a name I earned in fifth grade after I chopped off my braids so my catcher's mask would stop getting stuck in my hair. I wasn't making a statement—I just had games to win and no time for girly nonsense. Honestly, Karl got shit done.

And then, in college? That's when someone realized my initials were K.Y.

Yep. K.Y.

So of course I got tagged with the nickname "Jelly."

I embraced it and began my collection of stuffed jellyfishes. That nickname stuck for a while.

Not unlike the product.

I was lucky enough to grow up on a 100-acre farm in Liberty Mounds, just south of Tulsa, Oklahoma, along with my older sister, some older step-siblings that I could have lived without, their father (who was an excellent stepdad), and my badass of a mother. My biological parents divorced when I was two. My sister was six years older than me, but we were always very close and have been best friends throughout life. She picked on me almost every day of my life, and nothing could make her laugh harder than scaring the ever-living shit out of me. Amie would hide in our hallway just outside the bathroom door and wait for me to walk out. "MRRRRAHHHHH" is the sound she would make as I screamed my way into laughter, realizing my sister had done it again. Don't get me started on the time she told me the Incredible Hulk was in my closet. I'm talking Lou Ferrigno Hulk, not some CGI Mark Ruffalo the hottie Hulk. Amie instilled thick skin in a way only a loving older sister could do and was always in my corner. None of the older kids at my school picked on me because Amie would threaten to kick their asses, adding to my stupid bravery. Our Dad picked us up every weekend religiously until Amie could drive us to his house. I don't remember my dad ever missing a weekend. I always felt sorry for my cousins because their parents weren't divorced; *oh, how it must have sucked not to have two loving dads.* I was blessed with many close cousins from all sides of my family who lovingly picked on me since before I could walk, contributing more to my thick skin out of pure love.

My mom was a beast. Let it be known that neither one of these fathers were involved in purchasing the aforementioned magical plot of land in rural Oklahoma. My mother bought that 100-acre piece of heaven, and my stepdad, I am told, showed up with a suitcase. A jockey, basketball star, and Valedictorian in her former years, my mom was as sharp as she was tough. She would come home from her Executive Level bank job in downtown Tulsa, change out of her business suit/high heel getup and into her Wranglers and cowboy boots, and then she would hop on a tractor and brush hog our pasture until dark. Most notably, my mom wasn't afraid of a soul on this earth, and people truly adored the way my mother made them feel. She made me feel like I could do anything in the world and really encouraged me to find something I loved and slay at it. I couldn't decide on just one.

There were three things I loved doing when I got home from school:

1. Playing our old out-of-tune upright piano until my sister couldn't take it anymore.

2. Making ugly digital art on a pre-Windows computer to be

printed on a dot-matrix printer.

3. Pretending I was Janet Jackson.

Our land was on the end of a dead-end country road, and we couldn't see a neighbor's house from anywhere we stood. It was wooded, had a front and back pasture for my mother's horses, three ponds, a basketball court for my sister the hoops stud, an above-ground pool, a rodeo arena, two barns, and a productive colorful garden that my mom tended to regularly. Every day of my life, I cared for sheep, cattle, goats, chickens, peacocks, dogs that were the size of small Polar bears, and of course, horses. Every creature on our farm had a name, and was there solely to get fat and to live out its animal life being loved by my mother. I lived with a jockey, a barrel racer, and a true American cowboy and farrier, but I guess I wasn't born to be a horse whisperer. I never had a horse that wanted me on it, so they bought me a digital piano instead. To this day, it has never bucked me off.

Playing the piano has always been easy for me; some say it's because I'm ambidextrous. (or maybe I'm ambidextrous because of the piano?) I never understood why people thought I was talented in any way. I would hear a song I liked on the radio, sit down on a 60-year-old piano bench, and play my favorite New Kids on the Block song within a few minutes, complete with chords and melodies. At six years old, I began taking piano lessons from a high school student down the road. She had a massive crush on my step-brother, so she never missed a Wednesday. I took advantage of her passion for my manspreading sibling by marriage, asked her dozens of questions in our short 30-minute weekly session, and could mostly understand sheet music when I finished the first grade. I convinced my mom to fire Shianne, the piano teacher, because I wasn't happy playing the ridiculous songs about Clowns and Wigwams that were in my piano book, "Teaching Little Fingers to Play." I wanted to play songs on the radio, and did. There wasn't a song on mainstream radio I didn't know the words to. I had mix tapes that ran the gamut. From 80's Country to Gangster Rap, I loved it all. Pink Floyd songs were followed by Ice Cube. From Steve Miller to Queen, from the remixed raps of Snoop Dogg to the deep Oklahoma twang of Garth Brooks, music made me happy. Making music made me happy.

I wasn't afraid to ask questions, either. Some days if I was confused about an advanced time signature, I would bring my sheet music to school so my two best friends could dumb it down for me. I knew their moms wouldn't let them quit piano lessons in this lifetime and that they would be a treasure trove of information that I was deprived of due to my unstructured way of learning. They were always so patient with my questions. They would even come to my house and teach me for hours. Over the years, my mom put me in and pulled me out of lessons, but I hated them all. I didn't want to play in Carnegie Hall like my two best friends probably could have. I just wanted to play. I would invite other friends over, teach them songs on the piano, and make them play duets with me before we could go swimming. I knew they were there for the pool and my four-wheeler, so I dangled those things as carrots just to have someone to play the bass clef section of Heart and Soul. To this day, my favorite song to jam out to is "November Rain" by Guns & Roses, and legend has it that if you close your eyes, you could swear I was Axl Rose himself. I invested countless hours studying every beat of that song until I could play all nine minutes of it with my eyes closed. *Yes, I am entirely aware that playing the piano probably kept my mischievous, creative mind out of a lot of trouble.*

One childhood story that sticks out was when I was twelve years old, I literally smashed my face in half and kept going.

Let me explain.

I was riding the four-wheeler my dad bought me (my mom did NOT approve) down our long, dead-end county road with my friend Anita—helmetless, of course, like the little rebel I was, and letting her drive, which was a double no-no. I rode passenger on the back of my own four-wheeler, hollering encouragement like a tiny redneck life coach, telling her she could totally handle the curves. Anita promptly forgot to turn. She bailed. I didn't.

I was still sitting toward the back of that Yamaha quad when my face met a nine-inch steel pole—the one that held our driveway gate together. Full speed. Full face.

I remember thinking: *Well shit. That's gonna leave a mark.*

But here's the thing—I wasn't crying. I wasn't panicked. I wasn't even worried about my face. I was worried about my four-wheeler. If my mom found out we wrecked it, that sucker was gone. She wasn't happy when her ex-husband surprised me with this gift in the first place, and was constantly worried I would get hurt riding it. I could not let my mother know she was right all along.

So I went into action. Anita and I hauled the crooked, grass-stained and blood-soaked machine back to the house, veered straight past the front door, and parked it at the basketball court. While I painted Jackson Pollock-style blood splatters all over the concrete with my face, I sent Anita to rinse off the four-wheeler with my mom's garden hose. If my momma thought I broke my nose playing basketball, she couldn't take away a big ole slab of concrete. I would take the busted nose. I would take the black eyes. I would even take the eventual five surgeries to fix it.

But I would not lose my four-wheeler.

Turns out I crushed my nose. Crushed it. My face looked like I went three rounds with Mike Tyson, and I never let on how bad it hurt. That's the thing about growing up on a farm and being raised by a powerhouse mom—you learn early that grit isn't optional. It's survival.

And I didn't tell her the truth for over two decades. I finally came clean two days before she died, sitting beside her hospice bed, holding her hand. "Momma," I said, "I didn't break my nose playing basketball. I broke it on the four-wheeler."

She blinked slow and cracked a smile, and then the whole room—my stepdad, my aunts, everybody—just lost it. Laughed in absolute disbelief that I had held onto that lie for all those years, protecting my four-wheeler like it was a national treasure.

Even in her final days, my momma shook her head and grinned at me. "You little shit."

And she wasn't wrong.

Speaking of mischief, that's precisely what led to my graphic design career. The first few weeks of the sixth grade, I decided I would no longer be a good kid with good grades who was nice to my mom anymore. I stopped getting straight A's and only completed enough homework to pass this hormonal year with a D average. I was meticulous not to fail, but I wasn't trying to succeed either.

When I got my first D on a report card, I knew my momma's eyes would never see it. I thought fast and digitally recreated the school's report card, without any training, complete with a replica of the official school signatures, on software that was never designed to do so. I created this masterpiece three more times during my sixth-grade hellion spree, once every nine weeks. Hellion may not be the proper term. I was unapologetically Karrah at all times. Like the time I got a month of detention for taking my uncomfortable bra off in class and putting it in my gym bag. If Matt Anthony had kept his fat mouth shut, the bra would have quietly made it to my Nike gym bag, I would be reading my Social Studies book in total comfort, and all would be well with the world. Matt Anthony's version was that I slung my A cup brazier around in circles above my head like a birthday stripper. I didn't, but that didn't keep Matt Anthony from telling it that way. Fucker.

By the time my seventh-grade year rolled around, I had decided that I would use my computer art skills for good from that point forward and have. To quote Peter Parker, "with great power comes great responsibility." I decided to be a straight-A student again. I was even nice to my mom once more and mostly gave her the respect she deserved and commanded. *Now I could get in trouble for talking again.*

I was always a bit of an overachiever and had my hands in many activities in high school. I was an athlete, learned to weld, was typing around 110 wpm, and had to be great at everything I did. I had friends who were popular kids, nerds, bad kids, good kids, the country kids, and the country kids who thought they weren't country kids. We were all country kids seeing how our little town was composed of our K-12 school, a baptist church, a gas station where somebody could acquire cigarettes at any age, and a volunteer fire department. There weren't many students at my school I didn't connect with, being the talker that I was. It wasn't that difficult when you graduated with 32 people. I went to school for thirteen years with a good portion of my senior class, so most of them had grown to love my outgoingness, while a select few couldn't wait to start their new Karrah-free life. I typically just didn't trust people who chose not to like me. If they couldn't pick up on my genuine love of learning from everyone around me, I was pretty good about showing them the exit. I have always been aware that my personality takes up a lot of space some days. I learned to take a scowl from a bully as a challenge, knowing they would see the good in me in due time. I truly felt sorry for the few mean girls that crossed my path during my younger years. How horrible their home lives must have been to feel the need to squash my flame.

Over the course of my junior and senior year, I attended a vocational school in Tulsa on top of my high school curriculum. I was a certified Medical Office Assistant and Licensed Phlebotomist by the time I walked across the stage to receive my high school diploma. I wasn't Valedictorian like my mother was in high school, or Salutatorian like my sister was even, but I did play the piano while my class sang "This Used to be My Playground" by Madonna. My class was sharp. I graduated with straight As, just shy of a 4.0, with honors, and I barely made the top ten. I loved being the dumb one of this group of geniuses.

I also had a short-lived side hustle as a birthday party hostess at Chuck E. Cheese's during high school and on college breaks. Yes, I danced on stage. Yes, I sang the birthday song. And yes, sometimes I even suited up as the giant rat himself. There's something oddly eye opening about doing the robot dance in a musty rodent costume while a room full of sugared-up second graders screams at you like you're a god—*being an actual celebrity would suck.*

And listen—I wouldn't say I stole from my employer, but I definitely engaged in a little unsanctioned redistribution of joy. When I saw a kid whose family clearly couldn't afford enough tokens to earn the big prizes, I made sure they left with a giant stuffed animal anyway. Those ticket counters were basically kid capitalism at its worst, and I had a soft spot for the underdog. The managers probably suspected something, but I guess it's hard to accuse the dancing rat of embezzlement with a straight face.

After high school, I naively headed into the medical field, and I always felt it was my true calling to help people. My career as a frontline medical worker did not last long, though. After two years of waking up at 6 am and cussing at my thirty-mile drive in Tulsa rush hour traffic to study medical terminology, learning to stick people with needles, medical coding, and every skill needed to run a standard doctor's office, my medical career came to a screeching halt...

I saw an old lady's boobs.

Looking back, it wasn't her boobs that scared me off. It was the fact I couldn't bear wondering how vulnerable she must feel in the Skilled Nursing section of St. Francis Hospital with some clueless teenage stranger who has lost all her color. I was aching on the insides. That's all it took to get me to attend the University of Science and Arts of Oklahoma, where I studied mass communications.

I got in trouble for talking there too.

Leading up to the Great Silence of 2014, a few failed relationships, 27 hours of labor, one emergency C-Section and full hysterectomy later, I had gone from being a golden child with infinite possibilities to being a struggling single mother with two jobs on the brink of food stamps, who was down a uterus and a couple of ovaries. I had somehow gone from living on Heaven on Earth to a hideous rent house in a bad neighborhood. It seems I didn't actually have the world by its ass. I didn't need to anymore, I had my Rayne.

I was working for a locally owned music store in South Tulsa, where I was the graphic designer and also taught piano lessons. I loved teaching kids, but I specialized in Group Adult Beginner Piano Lessons, for the people who always wanted to learn how but were afraid. I taught groups of 5-10 adults at a time, four nights a week. My students ranged from lawyers, accountants, nurses, a former FBI agent, the Director of the Cherokee Gaming Commission, and even other musicians. I even taught a district judge, a wonderful lady that treated me like I was her daughter.

I wasn't there to teach them how to become professional pianists. I was there to give them the confidence to try to play an instrument because it just makes a person feel good to make music, and gosh did I love my students. They really loved me back hard too, and I genuinely looked forward to every class. I couldn't believe someone was paying me money to snap my fingers like a human metronome a few times a week! I finally had people to play the bass section of Heart and Soul with me. And they were paying me to be there.

I never set out to teach kids, but when a student was ready to quit after a tough experience with another teacher, the Lessons Coordinator would quietly add them to my schedule, hoping I could help them fall in love with music again. Turns out, she was right. One by one, they stayed. And slowly, my schedule filled with young musicians who connected with my relaxed, encouraging way of teaching—and reminded me just how special it is to be part of someone's musical beginning.

Rayne's father, while being an amazing partner to me although my pregnancy, unfortunately got hooked on the painkillers the hospital had given me for my C-Section. I couldn't take them because I wanted to be able to wake up when she cried, so I toughed it out. He didn't. By the time Rayne was two-years-old, she and I moved in with my elderly handicapped father to take care of him. So now my having the world by its ass has turned into being a single mother to my child born out of wedlock, and living with my Dad.

I was still very happy with my life. After all, I was paid to be peppy, and it wasn't tough to summon up the sunshine most days. Other than rehearsing Carol of the Bells during the weeks before Halloween, teaching piano is actually a very fun and rewarding job. The family that owned the music school where I taught were wonderful people. I was very lucky to supplement my single mom $13/hour income with dozens of paying piano students, which put me just above the food stamp cutoff. (While I truly believe in the welfare system, I was proud to not qualify for food stamps.) All I had to do was show up, be in a good mood, be motivational and encouraging, and snap my fingers on rhythm. That became impossible in October of 2014 when I met Jason Lewis.

I'm from a microgeneration most people don't even know exists—the Oregon Trail Generation. Or some people refer to us as "The Goonies." We were the kids caught between two worlds: born without the internet, but expected to master it by high school. We learned cursive and coding. We grew up with rotary phones, used payphones to call our parents after school, then learned to text on T9 and cheered for the new iPhone. We survived dial-up, floppy disks, and group science projects without Google. We played outside until the porch light came on, then stayed up late talking smack in AOL chatrooms on dial-up internet. We learned HTML to make our MySpace profiles sparkle. We didn't just watch the world change—we had to keep up, adapt, and reboot ourselves every time it did. That in-between upbringing shaped everything about me: the way I learn, the way I solve problems, the way I refuse to believe anything can't be figured out with a little curiosity and a lot of grit.

Looking back, I understand now that I was never just loud—I was wired for resistance. Every piano I played, every question I asked, every time I talked back in class or cracked a joke at the wrong moment... it was all practice. I didn't know I was being trained to survive, to challenge, to outsmart, to outlast. But I was.

And when the world tried to silence me, it didn't stand a chance.

Because this mouth?

It was born on a dead-end road in Oklahoma, fed by mixtapes, layered with mischief, and sharpened with age.

I'll keep using it until the story's done.

And as for the monster who tried to write my ending?

Poor thing never saw me coming.

He never stood a fucking chance.

Thelma & Louise 2.0

A poem by Karrah Youngblood

I never thought my mouth
Could get me into this much trouble.
I thought the cops would help me,
They quickly burst my bubble.
It's easier to believe a man, I guess—
It seems they're much more credible.
This made me find a spark within me,
And this new fire was spreadable.
I was ready to share my truth.
I would tell every journalist and editor
That the man who hurt me and so many others
Was a mean, methodical predator.
I teamed up with one of his victims,
And there were plenty there to choose from.

He hurt them bad with no remorse—
They were kidnapped, tortured, and then some.
The world needed to know he was a monster
That thrived off people's pain.
So I put his ugly face on a poster,
And then I made it rain.
We posted them at restaurants,
And schools and churches too.
We were spreading truth like Wildfire,
And there was nothing he could do.
We tried to warn the public
About this serial abuser
Being nothing but a conman—
A woman-beating loser.
It seems he didn't like his face
On every light pole in town.
So he sued me into silence,
But I refused to go down.
The judge ruled I was the villain here.
I was not allowed to speak his name.
But I don't have victims, Your Honor.
We are not the same.
Imagine my 441 days of silence.
Wrap your brain around that frustration.

Or learning a man plotting my death
Wasn't a protective order violation.
So now the story's being told
About his vicious ways.
Shutting me up didn't work for him—
Bitch, I can talk for days.
I'm still dancing in my kitchen.
And I'm still fierce and groovy.
I just hope Jennifer Lawrence
Plays me in the movie.

"Panic Button: Season 2 – Operation Wildfire"
created by Colleen McCarty and Leslie Briggs; produced by Oklahoma Appleseed Center for Law and Justice; distributed by The Panic Button Podcast;
℗ 2023 Oklahoma Appleseed Center for Law and Justice.

Select lyrics quoted in this work are the property of their respective copyright holders and are used under fair use for commentary and artistic expression.

"Bad Guy" written by Billie Eilish O'Connell and Finneas Baird O'Connell; performed by Billie Eilish; published by Universal Music Publishing Group, Last Frontier (ASCAP), and Kobalt Songs Music Publishing (ASCAP); ℗ 2019 Darkroom/Interscope Records.

"Bully" written by Brent Smith, Eric Bass, Zach Myers, and Barry Kerch; performed by Shinedown; published by EMI Blackwood Music Inc. and WC Music Corp.; ℗ 2012 Atlantic Recording Corporation (U.S.) / WEA International Inc. (outside U.S.).

"Comfortably Numb" written by Roger Waters and David Gilmour; performed by Pink Floyd; published by Pink Floyd Music Publishers Ltd.; ℗ 1979 Harvest Records.

"Go the Distance" written by Alan Menken and David Zippel; performed by Peyton Parrish; published by Walt Disney Music Company and Wonderland Music Company; ℗ 2021 Parrish Entertainment LLC (licensed to TuneCore).

"I Am Here" by P!nk (Written by Alecia Moore, Billy Mann, MoZella, Stephan Moccio, and Johan Carlsson) Published by EMI Blackwood Music Inc., Sony/ATV Songs LLC, and Pink Inside Publishing ℗ 2017 RCA Records, a division of Sony Music Entertainment.

"It Was a Good Day" written by O'Shea Jackson (Ice Cube), DJ Pooh, and Ronald Isley; performed by Ice Cube; published by Universal Music Publishing Group and EMI April Music Inc.; ℗ 1992 Priority Records, LLC.

"Learning to Fly" written by David Gilmour, Anthony Moore, Jon Carin, and Bob Ezrin; performed by Pink Floyd; published by Pink Floyd Music Ltd.; ℗ 1987 Pink Floyd Music Ltd. (under exclusive license to Sony Music Entertainment).

"Little Girl Gone" written by Chinchilla (Daisy Bertenshaw), Lewis Gardiner, and Mick Coogan Performed by Chinchilla. Published by Chinchilla Music / BMG Rights Management. ℗ 2023 Chinchilla Music under exclusive license to BMG Rights Management (UK) Ltd.

"Look What You Made Me Do" written by Taylor Swift, Jack Antonoff, Fred Fairbrass, Richard Fairbrass, and Rob Manzoli; performed by Taylor Swift; published by Universal Music Publishing Group / Sony/ATV; ℗ 2017 Republic Records.

"November Rain" written by W. Axl Rose; performed by Guns N' Roses; published by Universal Music Publishing Group; ℗ 1991 Geffen Records.

"One Little Soldier" written and performed by Regina Spektor; published by Sony/ATV Music Publishing; ℗ 2014 Regina Spektor Music.

"Praying" written by Kesha Sebert, Andrew Joslyn, Ben Abraham, and Ryan Lewis; performed by Kesha; published by Sony/ATV Music Publishing and Universal Music Publishing Group; ℗ 2017 Kemosabe Records / RCA Records.

"Rise" written by Katy Perry, Sarah Hudson, Max Martin, and Ali Payami; performed by Katy Perry; published by Warner Chappell Music, Universal Music Publishing Group; ℗ 2016 Capitol Records, LLC.

"Sister" written by Kristine Meredith Flaherty (K.Flay); performed by K.Flay; published by Warner Chappell Music; ℗ 2016 Interscope Records.

"Sound of Silence" written by Paul Simon; performed by Simon & Garfunkel (original) and Disturbed (cover); published by Paul Simon Music; ℗ 1964 Columbia Records (original), ℗ 2015 Reprise Records (Disturbed cover).

"Surefire" written by Max Rainer, Tyler Wimpee, and Justin Kila; performed by Wilderado; published by Bright Antenna Records; ℗ 2022 Bright Antenna, LLC.

"Take Me to Church" written by Andrew Hozier-Byrne; performed by Hozier; published by Sony/ATV Songs; ℗ 2013 Rubyworks Records.

"The Optimist" written by Evie Irie, Bryan Simpson, and Michael Fatkin; performed by Evie Irie; published by Kobalt Songs Music Publishing; ℗ 2024 Evie Irie / Kobalt Songs.

"The Phoenix" written by Patrick Stump, Pete Wentz, Joe Trohman, Andy Hurley, and Butch Walker; performed by Fall Out Boy; published by Universal Music Publishing Group; ℗ 2013 Island Records.

"Till I Collapse" written by Marshall Mathers and Luis Resto; performed by Eminem featuring Nate Dogg; published by Universal Music Publishing Group and Eight Mile Style; ℗ 2002 Aftermath Records / Shady Records / Interscope Records.

"Wildfire" written by Michael Martin Murphey and Larry Cansler. Performed by Michael Martin Murphey. Published by Sony/ATV Music Publishing LLC. ℗ 1975 Epic Records, a division of Sony Music Entertainment.

CHRISTEN
KARRAH
HEATHER
MARCI

#SpreadTheWildfire

For Survivor Resources, signed copies, or ways to help, visit

spreadthewildfire.com